WRITING FOR THE
DESIGN MIND

NATALIA ILYIN

WRITING · *for* *the* · DESIGN MIND

BLOOMSBURY VISUAL ARTS
LONDON • NEW YORK • OXFORD • NEW DELHI • SYDNEY

BLOOMSBURY VISUAL ARTS
Bloomsbury Publishing Plc
50 Bedford Square, London, WC1B 3DP, UK
1385 Broadway, New York, NY 10018, USA

BLOOMSBURY, BLOOMSBURY VISUAL ARTS and the Diana
logo are trademarks of Bloomsbury Publishing Plc

First published in Great Britain 2019

Cover design: Robert Baxter
Cover image © Robert Baxter

A catalogue record for this book is available from the British Library.

A catalog record for this book is available from the Library of Congress.

ISBN   PB   978-1-3500-3497-6
       ePDF   978-1-3500-3498-3
       eBook   978-1-3500-3499-0

Illustrated and designed by Robert Baxter

To find out more about our authors and books visit
www.bloomsbury.com and sign up for our newsletters.

for
Patrick F. Skinner
who taught many, many people to write,
including me

If you cannot write well, you cannot think well;
if you cannot think well, others will do your thinking for you.

OSCAR WILDE

Contents

LIST OF ILLUSTRATIONS

PREFACE

When an editor asked me if I would be interested in writing a book about writing, I felt very flattered and spent a few days practicing my book-signing signature. But after that, I had to take some time to think about the idea. I needed to figure out if another book about writing would be worth cutting down the trees. After all, *Writing Down the Bones* has been written; *If You Want to Write* has been written; *Bird by Bird* has been written. These are all wonderful books, and they'll teach you to write, if you're the kind of person who feels comfortable with words.

But my design students usually aren't that comfortable with words. They're generally visual creatures, and most books about writing aren't written for people whose primary experience of life is through their eyes. Many of my students get most of their sensory input visually and have spent much of their lives honing their skills in line, form, composition, and pattern, letting their verbal skills idle along at an unremarkable rate.

Are you a visual creature? Do you avoid walking past a certain house because the mint green of the walls clashes with the yellow-green of the trim? Do you cover your cookbooks because you can't stand a clash of typefaces in your kitchen bookcase? Do you refuse to go to a certain restaurant because the menu type style is Curlz? If any of this sounds familiar, I wrote this book for you.

Acknowledgments

Books are team efforts, and I am very lucky to have wonderful people on my team:

Cullen Stanley, my literary agent, who again provided the wise support she has lent to all my projects.

Louise Baird-Smith, who made sure that I had what I needed to get this manuscript out of my mind and onto the page. I so appreciate her unfailing good humor and common sense; she's made the whole process enjoyable, which is saying something.

Robert Baxter, who designed the book, its cover, and all its diagrams. Robert acted as designer, typographer, illustrator, illustration researcher, and sounding board—he went so many extra miles that I lost count of them.

Anna Ilyin McClain, who listened to and gave advice on many long and rambling ideas while also acting as chief nutritional advisor and therapist; Nadia Ilyin Mote, who found herself editing the beginning as I was writing the end of the same shared document, which felt a bit like we were playing Mozart's "Sonata for Two Pianos" on one keyboard; Alexandra Ilyin, who once again allowed me to use her life experiences as fodder. I know she's tired of this, and promise to exclude her from future books. Not really.

Elisabeth Patterson, my co-instructor in Design History and Criticism at Cornish College of the Arts, who took on many extra work hours and onerous tasks with her typical enthusiasm so that I could finish this book;

Dr. William Spencer, who parsed Kandinsky's musical metaphors for us; Maria V. Sokolova, who translated long, difficult English sentences into long, difficult Russian sentences with lightning speed;

My design and administrative colleagues, who inspire and energize me every time we meet: Jeff Brice, Tiffany Laine DeMott, Jake Fleischer, Jacob Kohn, Andrea

Leksen, Sarah Lenoue, and Chris Williams at Cornish College of the Arts; and Matt Monk, Jenn Renko, Tasheka Arceneaux-Sutton, Lorena Howard-Sheridan, Nikki Juen, Yoon Soo Lee, Ian Lynam, Ziddi Msangi, Silas Munro, David Peacock, Sereina Rothenberger, David Schatz, and Anne West at Vermont College of Fine Arts;

Kristin Von Kreisler (my Esteemed Relative), Gisele Fitch, Rick Barrenger, and Therese Caouette, all of whom forgave terrible social gaffes and stupidities caused by my getting absorbed in the manuscript and forgetting I was supposed to be somewhere;

And everyone at Cups, my local coffee place, who made me pot upon pot of decaf in the last stage of writing this manuscript and provided a wonderful place to think.

Thank you all!

INTRODUCTION
If You've Never Written

Since you're reading this, I imagine you're a designer who'd like to write. You may *want* to write—you have thoughts you want to get out into the world. Or you may *need* to write—someone wants something from you and you need to do a good job. Either way, the pressure's on.

You may like to read. Many designers actually do quite a bit of reading, between a blog here and a monograph there. But if you turn pale at the thought of *writing*, if you find yourself going to get coffee and then spending an inordinate amount of time judging the comparative design merits of the new Starbucks holiday mugs instead of going back and getting down to the task at hand, it's time to get serious and learn. You *can* learn to write well, and this book will teach you, if you do all the things I ask you to do.

I'm betting that, if you feel worried about writing, you never had a lot of practice in the basics in your early years in school. Perhaps no one had the chance to drill various grammatical niceties into you when you were young, and you didn't have the time to dedicate yourself to learning them later, what with all that getting up to speed on InDesign and Illustrator, or SketchUp, or CAD.

Maybe you did learn some basic writing skills along the way, or you write in a journal or blog a bit, but you aren't sure how to go about producing something bigger: a longer piece for a client or colleague, an article or academic piece about something you really care about. In these situations, the stakes are higher than usual and your writing needs to be clear, expressive, and—most important—under your control.

If you want to write but seem never to get down to it, you may be blocked. You may have always wanted to write as well as design, but when you were an impressionable teen, Mrs. Duxworthy of the Birkenstocks-with-Socks scoffed at your spelling and said that you'd better stick to drawing because you couldn't write your way out of a paper bag. And so—big surprise—you never wrote. You stuck to design and never looked over the big fence separating writing from designing, until now.[1]

I'm glad you've decided to look over that fence and at the wide world of writing beyond. I say scramble up and over: Writing well is a skill that will make your life better. If you can write exactly what you mean, you have the edge on those who cannot. Writing well means that you know how to structure your thoughts, choose your words, and bring people along into your ideas with you.

Writing is organized thinking put down on the page. Many people spend their lives not being able to define thoughts for themselves. Because they haven't learned how to do so, they have no choice but to leave the clear thinking to others. Because they cannot argue or persuade in their writing, they abdicate their verbal power. When you learn to write well you enter into life more deeply, because you can think a problem through, make a point, trace an experience, invent a world—and communicate it.

If you name your three favorite well-known designers, chances are that they write well. If they didn't, you probably wouldn't have heard of them. These are the designers who write proposals that convince important clients. They write design briefs that get the best out of their collaborators. They're always writing a little something in this blog or in that magazine. They write books about their work; they write books about other people's work. They write pieces that are clear, literate—often funny, sometimes poetic. Since they can write, they frame the wider design conversation. Other designers talk about the ideas these designers put forward. Because they're publishing, they become well known. This helps clients find them. These clients accept their well-written proposals—the spiral goes upward.

I've taught many designers to write, and most of them started with some common prejudices about their own talents and abilities. Let me guess a few things about you.

I'll bet that sometimes you feel guilty for not writing well. You think you should be good at it by now. Guilt is a fine thing, but it's not useful here. When you started designing, did you design well? Those first horrible cereal box designs

---

1   Spelling is not writing. W. B. Yeats, one of the greatest of modern poets, spelled terribly.

that you made when learning InDesign—do you want them in your portfolio? How about when you first drew, did you draw well? How many hours did you spent doodling anime characters in the seventh grade and logos in the ninth? You spent hours and hours. When you first drove a car, did you drive well? We shall not mention the nail marks on the passenger side left from the driving lesson during which your father grabbed the dashboard so hard he punctured the vinyl.

I shall never understand why people assume that they should be able to write like Michael Bierut or Gail Anderson or Kenneth FitzGerald the first time they write anything. These well-known designers have practiced their writing for a long, long time. Their first efforts were probably stiff, wordy, and dull. But they kept practicing, kept going, and became wonderful writers. Let the guilt go: You're here now.

Here's another thing about you. "Oh, you're so *visual*!" your teachers may have chorused in days gone by. "You're so *right-brained*!" And then, under their breath, "You'll never be good at math or writing."

I hate this. I hate everything about this. I cannot tell you how many times I have heard instructors say this kind of thing to students, and how many times students have echoed this false bit of insight about themselves back to me. When I hear it, I get so annoyed that I start glowering at the instructor over the head of the student, or glowering at the student over the heads of the other students. This makes for a nice educational atmosphere.

Where did we get the idea that being "visual" means you can't be "verbal?" Did Vincent van Gogh avoid writing profound letters to his brother because he was a painter?[2] Did Leonardo da Vinci sit up one day and say, "Uh, wait, I guess I shouldn't be writing down my ideas on human anatomy, war machines, the creation of the world, painting, plants, how human bodies work, proportion, perspective, architecture, geography, or zoology because I'm *visual, not verbal*."

No. He did not sit up one day and say this.

There's a simple explanation for this black-and-white "visual or verbal" teaching error. When you and your contemporaries were going to grade school, a fad in the education of the time promoted the idea that people were either visual learners or verbal learners. Teachers were supposed to figure out which bucket you fell into, and take it from there. It naturally followed, as the night the day, that teachers fell

2   Van Gogh said, "If you hear a voice within you say 'you cannot paint,' then by all means paint … and that voice will be silenced."

into the habit of thinking you had no aptitude for the other set of skills. You just didn't have the brain for it, so the story went.

This visual-or-verbal idea made a lot of sense to instructors, because all students tend to lean more toward one thing than the other. But it's faulty thinking, and it was promoted by poorly-tested psychological research. Luckily, in the last decade, the idea that your hardwired talent lands you in the visual department or the verbal department has been disproved, but an entire system of educational learning relies on the concept, and it'll take a while for educational systems to catch up.[3]

So that's the situation with "visual" vs. "verbal." But what about that other thing people say you are: *left-brained* or *right-brained*? "You're so right-brained!" they've told you. Another reason you may have been given a pass on learning to write well. Let's take a look at this old chestnut.

People like to think of creative people as "right-brained" (thinking holistically, intuitively, using motor skills, visualization, and imagination) rather than "left-brained"(thinking hierarchically, logically, sequentially, with words and with facts). But these days, cognitive scientists believe that different places all over the brain become active during complex functions, and they don't really believe the "left-" and "right-" brain idea anymore. Its day has passed.[4]

LEFT ——— RIGHT

fig 0.1
The left and right knot.

It turns out that "visual creatures" have much more in common with writers and theoretical physicists and engineers than many people could have imagined. Systems thinking, an area of exploration in science and the humanities, works better for describing the creative mind than do either/or, black-and-white approaches.[5] Artists, designers, and writers have minds attuned to recognizing

---

3 http://healthland.time.com/2009/12/28/can-people-really-be-visual-or-verbal-learners/
4 Dividing people up into left- or right-brained might have been an unconscious effort to name which of the two opposing forces of human consciousness had their hold upon the individual at hand. Interesting as an idea, but metaphorical, not scientific.
5 "So what is a system? A system is a set of things—people, cells, molecules or whatever—interconnected in such a way that they produce a pattern of behavior over time. The system may be buffeted, constricted, triggered, or driven by outside forces. But the system's response to these forces is characteristic of itself, and that response is seldom simple in the real world."
Donella Meadows, *Thinking in Systems*

patterns and creating systems of meaning, and they understand these systems in many of the same ways that engineers and physicists do.

If you're attracted to being a designer, it's likely that you have an affinity for systems thinking, and, without realizing it, you've spent your life training your mind to take advantage of this affinity. Of course, there are people in the world who *are* ruled by artistic impulse, just as there are people who are ruled by hierarchical thinking. But the idea that all "right-brained" people are "artistic," and therefore unsuited to hierarchical thinking, has limited the societal value of the work of artists and designers during the last 200 years, during the rise of industry and technology.

Describing people as unsuited to a particular kind of thinking devalues them and their contributions to culture. So, before describing yourself as "right-brained," or "visual rather than verbal," make sure you're not merely adopting labels people have invented to reduce your power and agency in the world.

Lots of students who steer a course toward design do so because they're dyslexic (like many of my students) and have found art classes, and drawing in particular, to be a way out of the pain of not being able to read easily in a society that depends upon reading as its main form of instruction. From a distance, drawing can look like a way into a career that doesn't require a lot of reading and writing. But an education in illustration or design does not bear out this assumption. If you're an illustrator or designer, you'll write contracts, proposals, emails, briefs on research, and the occasional article.

About the time that students get into their second year of college, they find themselves writing quite a bit, and this is difficult for those who chose the profession to avoid reading and writing. If this describes your situation, remain calm. When your teachers begin to give you writing assignments, don't curl into a small ball and avoid them, preferring instead to work on your dragon-drawing, hoping the whole writing thing will disappear in a puff of pink smoke. With the skills this book teaches, you'll become the dragon and your fire-breath shall charbroil avoidance.

If you're dyslexic and bracing for yet another bout of confusion as we get to the crux of the learning, let me lay your fears to rest. This book is more about finding relationships among ideas, strategizing ways to get them out, and patterning their sequencing than it is about spelling or micro-editing. Yes, we'll talk briefly about some basic grammar and syntax without which you cannot move ahead, but mostly we'll concentrate on drawing out your ideas—which is just up your alley. So, forge ahead with the exercises, pattern them out, go as far as you can go, and if you're in school, dust off your accommodations and work closely with your instructor. If you're doing this on your own, find a good copyeditor to work with you as you get to the final stages of your writing project's development.[6] As Edsger W. Dijkstra said, "Do only what only *you* can do."[7] Get the ideas down that only you have. You'll find good people to work with you on the finishing touches.

Whether you want to take your rightful place in the creation of a future that is humane and just and equal or you would just like to make a ton of money and buy a cottage overlooking the ocean, you need to know how to get your ideas clearly, beautifully, and convincingly onto the page. Personal power lies in the ability to produce written argument.

Tough it out through all the exercises. If you don't complete them, don't expect much in the way of improvement. It's a one-two punch. Read the chapter, do the exercises. And let me know how it goes.

Many good wishes,

NATALIA ILYIN
In earpods, over the Great Lakes

---

6   I don't advise the use of writing apps. Currently, these apps are rule-based and do not adapt to the subject at hand or to your writing style. This can result in tepid prose and outright errors. Perhaps more important, these apps are designed to promote your dependency upon them so that you'll continue to use them, and so their developers can continue to monetize your lack of knowledge. Dependency is not a creative advantage.

7   Edsger Dijkstra, one of the inventors of computer science, insisted that code be elegant. He also said, and I concur, "If 10 years from now, when you are doing something quick and dirty, you suddenly visualize that I am looking over your shoulders and say to yourself, 'Dijkstra would not have liked this,' well, that would be enough immortality for me."

CHAPTER ONE

Sitting Down to Write

WHEN WE START TO WORK TOGETHER, my design students sometimes feel embarrassed about how hard it is for them to write an academic paper or a professional-sounding email. They seem to think that writing should come naturally to them, the way it comes naturally to their roommate who *just loves* to write in her journal. They see her in her cozy robe and slippers, listening to music, pausing now and then to check her phone, spending Saturday morning letting the words flow effortlessly from her gel pen. They hear her say chirpy things like, "I could just write, write, write all day," as she makes herself another latte in the kitchen.

"What's wrong with me," my students' doleful expressions seem to say. "Why can't I get comfy and just *write, write, write* the way my journaling roommate does? She has a wonderful time pouring out her thoughts, while I sit staring at my laptop waiting for words to come, feeling my body set like ready-mix concrete."

First, let me put your mind at rest. Writing should not come easily to you. If it comes easily to you, it's probably not very good writing. This roommate of yours may enjoy getting her deepest feelings onto the page. She may be fully engaged in her journaling. But that does not make her a *writer*. Journaling is a process in which the unconscious is given free play and throws anything it feels like throwing out onto the page. Journaling can set a person up for writing by unearthing unconscious material and it can clear the detritus of the everyday so that deeper thoughts can surface. But journaling itself is not *writing*. You journal for yourself—to get stuff out of yourself. You write for other people.

Although you can journal in a robe and fuzzy slippers, I don't recommend you write in them. Getting too cozy will work against you. As in other areas of life, balance is key. Uncomfortable, and you won't focus. Too comfy, and you'll be snoring before long. Mental and physical comfort is not required to write well. Dante Alighieri wrote the *Divine Comedy* as a refugee, "while sitting on his bench in Ravenna," after having been thrown out of his hometown of Florence. Solzhenitsyn wrote his first novel in a Soviet prison camp, constructing long parts of his book in his memory, waiting for a time that he could put it all down when he got some paper. And Walter Benjamin wrote some of his finest criticism while hiding in friends' basements, on the run from the Nazis.[8] So don't worry that you need to get comfortable before you start to write. What you need is a situation in which you're able to focus. Pilots do not fly in lounge chairs, but they don't sit on stools either. When we get to the exercises, we'll talk about how to set up your writing space for optimum concentration.

TEN THINGS ABOUT WRITING

Up front, I want to mention ten things. I've found that students don't mind hearing that something is going to be hard to do—but they mind very much if someone says things are going to be casual and fun and then they turn out to be difficult and complex. I think you'd rather know what's up ahead than start to get creepy notions of personal deficiency if the work begins to feel difficult. So here are ten challenges of writing well. You'll find your way around each one of them.

— 1   *The structures of writing are invisible.*

When you're designing, you're generally given the content, and InDesign or SketchUp or whatever allows you to see the pages and the type and images or the walls and rugs and wood grains that you're choosing to create the form of the piece. You make design decisions and immediately know how the whole piece is being affected. But writers create the *form* of the piece at the same time that they create the *content*. They create the wine glass and the wine at the same time. Tricks make it easier.

---

8   Walter Benjamin wrote *Art in the Age of Mechanical Reproduction*, a classic design school critical text. A well-known Jewish intellectual, he was marked for death by the Nazis. During all his days and nights on the run, he wrote feverishly. He had ideas to get out, and he fought to get them out before his inevitable arrest.

Many writing teachers use outlining as a method for capturing and structuring writing so that you don't have to keep that wineglass-of-form in your head as you're creating the wine of your argument or idea. I never enjoyed outlining—it feels too wordy and I always had to think too much about Roman numerals and what "IX" and "VII" meant, and I hate the confinement of knowing what I'm going to say before I say it, so I generally find myself sketching out the structure of what I am going to write before I write it. I also teach my students to sketch the wineglass out. You will be trying this shortly.

— 2   *Writing is rewriting.*

Even when you become a very good writer, writing will never be like a drift of rose petals floating from your mind down to the page. As a matter of fact, the better you get, the less it will be a drift of petals and the more it will be like carrying a piano upstairs. But once the piano is upstairs you will lie upon it in your best sequins and toast yourself with triumph.

Real writing is rewriting. When you get good, you'll sketch out a few arguments, write a first draft, rework the sketch, write a second draft, and find, at the end of a three-hour stint of being hard at writing that second draft, that you've lost 200 words in your word-count. This does not feel good when you're writing against a deadline or when you're trying to get up to that page count your instructor expects. But when this shrinkage happens to you, do not get disgusted and fling things about. Congratulate yourself. Fewer words after working means you're honing, not journaling. And most important, it means you're really writing. It means that people are going to want to read what you've written because you're not flinging rose petals at them. You're not stuffing your sentences with extra words and pompous jargon. Rewriting shows respect for the reader.

— 3   *Writing requires your full attention.*

The time you use for writing cannot be fractured and half-attended and chopped up, in the ways we usually spend our days. As a designer, you may be used to handling a number of projects at once and working in a buzzy, caffeinated state answering various vibrations and dings and checking the news headlines to see what got blown up in the last hour. But writing well requires focus. Most writers have to practice *disengagement* in order to write. It takes mental effort to reduce the chatter in your mind, turn off the phone, avoid checking email, stop ruminating about other projects, stop thinking about whether you have something in the refrigerator that you can make for dinner, about whether you need to buy dog treats, or if you turned off the coffeemaker. Writing is a meditative act. And as such, these days, it is a radical act of self-value and self-control.

— 4   *Writing requires that you be dead honest with yourself.*

Though you may wear a mask or don a persona for your reader, you cannot mask your ideas from yourself. You'll be surprised at how often your brain will try to hide what it really wants to say from your writing mind. Sometimes you'll feel as though you're caught in a mental Dance of the Seven Veils,[9] trying to figure out what lies under all the first efforts at getting it down on the page, the anxiety, the procrastination, and the avoidance.

Just pull off one veil at a time. The idea will appear at last, in all its hard-won beauty. You must puzzle out what your unconscious wants to say in the piece you're writing, because your readers will stop reading if they begin to feel that tinny feeling that you don't know what you're writing toward.[10] They don't want to organize a big pile of veils for you: You have to do it. Intellectual integrity is demanding. It requires that you think clearly and find appropriate ways to communicate. Getting a true idea down is a victory.

— 5   *Writing well courts risk.*

Writing poorly requires nothing from you because few people will have the stamina to read what you wrote. You don't care, they don't care—it's a not-caring festival of nothing. But writing well requires mental toughness, because when you

---

9   The Babylonian goddess Ishtar "performed the first documented striptease" when she descended into the underworld in search of Tammuz. Ishtar must "relinquish her jewels and robes at each of the seven gates to the underworld until she stands naked in the "land of no return." Oscar Wilde assigned this symbolic descent to the underworld of the unconscious, a ceremony that equates stripping naked to being in a state of truth, the ultimate unveiling, to Salome." Toni Bentley, *Sisters of Salome* (Lincoln: University of Nebraska Press, 2005), 30–36.

10 Please don't assume that your unconscious mind's unedited wanderings make for delightful reading. James Joyce and Jack Kerouac may inspire you toward these efforts, but in fact both authors knew quite a bit about form before they started deconstructing their writing. Under *Finnegan's Wake* and *On the Road* lies a foundation of compositional knowledge not unlike trestles under the Long Island Railroad.

CHAOTIC SURFACE   **UNDERLYING STRUCTURE**

get your well-written ideas out there, someone's going to read what you wrote and then criticize it.

I'm not talking about an editor suggesting changes for clarity or about the usual barrage of trolling that everyone gets these days if they raise their heads above the bog-level of the Internet and state an opinion. I'm talking about criticism from professional critics; people who mean something in the profession and who will take you on and push you intellectually about the content of your piece. Being taken seriously can be a difficult adjustment.

Students often come in thinking that the word "criticism" means finding fault with something, looking for the weak spots, finding something harsh to say. That's the common use of the word. But "criticism" in design and in writing is not that: It's trying to figure out what problem the writer or designer has set up and then deciding whether the writer or designer solved the problem. On a larger scale, criticism is a discussion of how the piece of design or writing fits into the cultural context. What does the design tell us about what's going on today in design? How does the written piece reflect design values that we share today that may not have been design values we shared yesterday?

Criticism is never anyone's favorite thing. But soon you'll treat criticism of your writing in the same way you treat critique of your designing. You'll consider the source. You'll know that real criticism—criticism that points something out that you may have missed or makes a connection that you didn't see—is of *immense value*. This kind of criticism gets you further in your thinking, quickly. But bad criticism—vague hand-waving about how you just generally didn't hit the mark in some unexplained way—is laziness on the part of the "critic" and is worthless to you.

Trash anything vague, anything snarky, and anything that doesn't spell out what the issue is exactly and what you did or did not do. Ignore the lackluster critic's favorite phrase, "They could have pushed their ideas further," which means absolutely nothing. For criticism to be valuable, the person criticizing you must puzzle out what you're trying to do, then find particular ways in which you did or did not achieve your objective. If you're lucky, someday someone will read your work closely enough to deliver this kind of opinion.

— 6 *Writing well takes time.*

A very large amount of time. Ask me how I know. Writing can take a big chunk out of your day—a weekday already filled with client work, classes, meetings, email, and commuting—or a weekend day already planned for making food, scrubbing floors, doing laundry, working out, catching up with work, seeing family and friends, and taking the odd shower. You must schedule writing in, because it won't fit easily into your calendar. And you'll never get as much done as you think you will. Aim for 500 good words a day. If you talk into a voice recognition app and the transcript is 5,000 words, hone it down to the 500 you really needed.

— 7 *Writing guilt is not your friend.*

Writing guilt hits design students and design academics because they're under a lot of pressure to research and write—and, in the case of the academics, to publish. Sometimes they feel they should be writing at every moment that they're not teaching or being taught, and because of this pressure they find themselves procrastinating, then forcing themselves to stay at the desk for twelve hours, coming up exhausted and dry and behind schedule. Please do not do these things. They are disrespectful to your body and to your mind.

If you remember one thing from this book, please remember this: Write from a place of health. Do not go without sleep, food, contact with friends, a look at a tree or a leaf, a spate of love, or the petting of dogs. There's nothing noble about being a tortured artist. There's no percentage in it. Lashing yourself to the desk is not going to work long-term and you have better ways to spend your time on the planet.

If you sit down to write but the words aren't coming, get up, get out, and go check the sprinkler or something. Breathe some air and repot a geranium, then come back and try again. If again nothing comes to you after another twenty minutes, quit again. Scrub the kitchen floor. An idea may occur to you when you're sloshing around with the bucket and the Murphy's Oil. Get up, go to your desk, and put that idea down. The most successful writing practice is the one you can work into your everyday life without building up too much pressure on yourself or dissolving into a puddle of ease. Just make writing another thing you do, like repotting a plant or scrubbing a floor.

Writing guilt happens to professional designers, too. When I talk with an audience, designers often come up to me afterward and say sheepishly that they know they should be writing. Nothing could be further from the truth. Why should designers write unless they have something to say that cannot be said with the objects they make? Not all professionals must write. But if you write, your career will be wider and deeper, and if you want it to be wider and deeper, well, then, that's another question, isn't it? We all want to excel at everything we do, even at things we don't naturally want to do. Examine your motives, decide if you really want to write, and then, if you do, get yourself entirely behind the work and push.

— 8   *Writing dissolves anxiety.*

Thinking about how you should be writing, or that you aren't good enough, or that someone will hate what you write, or that your instructor will give you a bad grade, or that you don't know where to start, can cause your mind to go in on itself in a way that can leave you a frozen ice sculpture of anxiety. Given that these are anxious times (though most times are anxious in one way or another) and that I have never had more students with accommodations for anxiety, I think it's a good idea here to mention the care of your mind.

An overwhelming sense of panic, anxious perspiration, rapid heartbeat? Urban life is a lot for the old reptilian brain to handle. If you want to write, you must take responsibility for your mind's care: No one else will. If you want to have real ideas, you must guard your one and only brain from too much input, keep it from too many zombie movies, too many endless games, too much bright color, too much loud sound, too many advertisements, too much alcohol, too much smoke, too much caffeine. Give it blocks of time without the phone, wrap it in cozy winter hats, be its protector.[11]

Most designers are sensitive people, and many live in charged, political, gritty atmospheres. This amps the hormone cortisol. Cortisol chews away at your bones and depresses your immune system. It shows up when you haven't eaten and when you're being chased by a deadline. It rockets anxiety, and it messes with your mind.

Anxiety is fear. What each of us fears is a personal cocktail, and the salves we use to pass through it are individual and unique. Yet I have stumbled upon a Great Truth: *When you sit down to write, the act of writing itself will calm and recenter you.* No matter how bad you feel, getting into the flow of your writing will make you feel better.

---

11   Born almost 2000 years ago, Epictetus was a Stoic. In his *Art of Living*, he said, "Most of what passes for legitimate entertainment is inferior or foolish and only caters to or exploits people's weaknesses. Avoid being one of the mob who indulges in such pastimes. Your life is too short and you have important things to do. Be discriminating about what images and ideas you permit into your mind. If you yourself don't choose what thoughts and images you expose yourself to, someone else will, and their motives may not be the highest. It is the easiest thing in the world to slide imperceptibly into vulgarity. But there's no need for that to happen if you determine not to waste your time and attention on mindless pap." Some advice does not age.

One minute, my student is clenching her fists and yawning with anxiety, the next she's focused and free, because she's got her mind on her writing and is absorbed in it. Try it. You'll be surprised. Just follow the basic routine for writing practice, which you'll soon read. Get your head down into the work and forget about everything else. Concentration is the greatest release from fear you'll ever find. "Flow" is a state of total engagement—it's time without fear.

How to get into the flow of writing? It's similar to the ways you get into the flow of designing. I'm betting you already have ways of signaling your brain that you're going to start in on the day's design work. Do you make some ramen, talk with your desk mate, listen to a particular song, then ease into thinking about the task at hand? These activities signal your reptilian brain that it's safe, that it can relax its grip, that your frontal lobes can start translating ideas into design, and that your amygdala doesn't have to be on red alert.

No need to fear that a lion is approaching the campsite, because your food and music and friendly gossip tell your brain that it's protected. Other humans are near; the communal voice of music sounds; you have food (symbolized by that bowl of noodles), so starvation isn't imminent—you can relax into designing. Easing into writing is similar. Physical routine lulls your mind into releasing itself from the everyday world.

— 9   *Noise is your enemy.*

The sound of a television, of your child's video game, the drone of a leaf blower, loud people in the coffee shop? Find yourself some earplugs. Or, if you're loaded with cash, buy some noise-canceling earbuds, which I desired for years, for which I finally sprung at an airport, and which I am currently wearing on a plane. They put the entire world in the background and bathe me in Zen-like tranquility until I've written what I need to write. Sometimes I forget I'm wearing them and people pound on my front door while I go around whistling a happy tune. I need to resolve this.

— 10   *False critics must go to the home.*

Say you've metabolized these last nine things. Feeling good, you decide you'll write. But suddenly, you're not alone. That famous writer you took a workshop from is looking over your shoulder, reminding you that she told you your poetry was horrible, so why try to write again? And here's the celebrated corporate designer from whom you so wanted that copywriting internship, scanning your work quickly and saying, "You look like a nice girl. Why don't you go home and get married?"[12] Ah yes, here they all are, gathered in a festive cluster around your desk. All the false critics who landed blows upon your unprotected head.

Anyone with any talent has received false "criticism" from people who buttress their egos by denigrating someone else, usually a younger person. (These people deserve to burn in Hell. Sadly, the underworld is not my jurisdiction.) The comments of false critics don't go away, but tend to swirl about and gather energy at important moments of creation. To end the pain, try this trick I learned from my old friend Burt, who's silenced a few self-proclaimed "experts" in his day.

Close your eyes and summon an image of the person who said the cruel thing. Smile warmly. Take that imagined person's arm and say, "Remember that comment you made about my work? It caused me great suffering. But now it's time for you and your comment to stop taking up room in my brain. I have reserved you a place at the lovely False Critics' Retirement Home, where you will spend the rest of your days in the company of other false critics. Sitting in a jarringly colorful garden, surrounded by a very tall wall, you'll enjoy excoriating the macaroni crafts of others while waiting for your four o'clock dinner to begin."

Envision yourself walking the false critic to the very tall gate, giving the false critic over to a friendly facilities assistant, closing the gate with a heavy clang, and walking back to a kinder reality.

Some false critics are shape-shifters. Their words may seem as though they're coming from your own mind, but if you close your eyes and really listen, you'll start to recognize the voice as belonging to someone from your past, someone who hit you when you didn't have the ego-strength to resist the punch. Whose voice is it? Stay focused and soon the face of the false critic will surface. Follow the steps above. Escort this shade to the False Critics' Retirement Home. Come back here, afterwards.

It's important to remember that people who enjoy demoralizing young or beginning writers—or demoralizing anyone, really—are not bona fide "critics." They're people who are unhappy with themselves, or who are afraid of you because you're young, or they don't understand who you are, or they cannot follow your thinking, which makes them feel stupid. They believe that if you get out of hand you might be a threat to their power. And so, they belittle you to reduce your power. Humans are mammals, not angels.

---

12 Yes, a famous corporate designer once said this to me. He is dead. Coincidence?

Your body and mind only want the best for you. Don't make them work under the brutal conditions someone else seeks to impose. Once you begin taking false critics to the home, your whole being will start to feel lighter. Trust yourself. Deep down your mind wants to get its truth out. Help it.

THE EXERCISES
How to Begin

Here's a little something about the exercises: They've been tweaked for years, they're time-tested, and they work. Try to avoid the designer's malady of thinking that you've instantly found a way to improve the process I'm about to describe. Don't suggest a streamlined version or offer a hack just yet. Hold off on the innovations until you've finished the entire process. And if we meet sometime, please don't tell me you loved this book (when you skimmed it at the bookstore) but of course you didn't do any of the exercises (because you're so terribly busy) and that (oddly) your writing didn't improve. If you say these words to me, I will pull a large club out of my purse and chase you around the bookstore. Either jump into this process with both feet or buy another book and spend more of your life not learning to write well.

Practice writing three times a week for a month. If life gets in your way and you can't show up at the chair one day, don't spend time punching yourself about it, just instantly forget it, the way you would instantly forget making an error in baseball so that you're ready for the next play. Show up at the chair on your next planned day. Make a little schedule so you can check off days. This check-off is very satisfying.

First, find a good chunk of time to write. My friend Sara-Lynne writes for an hour at 5:00 a.m. every day before her kids get up. It works for her, but it sounds awful to me. I find I write best in the time between putting dinner into the oven and getting it onto the table. I have a favorite chair near the kitchen, and I know my writing session will end when the oven timer sounds, so I tend to relax there and really write. The only downside here is that sometimes I get so caught up in the writing that I don't hear the timer's buzz, and dinner turns out a bit crispy. So, find forty minutes that are convenient for you, and that you can repeat three times a week. Habit is the key to production.

Second, organize your workspace. You need a solid table that you can lean on and a comfortable chair. Not a soft, relaxing chair—a supportive work chair. Mary

Heaton Vorse used to say that the art of writing is "applying the seat of the pants to the seat of the chair." Get a lumbar pillow for the chair. Clear and clean your new writing table. Then put a thick, fresh spiral notebook and your lucky pen on the table, along with your copy of this book and an old-fashioned kitchen timer. (No expensive journals! Just an 8.5" × 11" spiral notebook.) Nothing else on the table, unless you need a lamp.

Make sure you'll be warm enough. Drape a throw around your shoulders if it's winter. Direct a light breeze toward yourself if it's summer. For now, plan to show up for forty minutes. (Don't use your computer for writing yet. You'll get back to it later.) A few minutes before your writing practice time comes, set up a pot of tea and warm a good mug. If you're going to be a writer you're going to need a good mug.

Banish your phone to another room or you'll end up checking Instagram. Don your ear buds if you think you need complete silence. (I actually concentrate best when there are people somewhere near—but not too near.) Don't listen to music while you're writing. Writing has its own music, and you don't want the conflict of two types of music in your brain.

Sit down at the desk, and, timing yourself, take five minutes to clear your mind of distractions. You might focus on a dot on the wall or on a favorite object, or use a short, guided meditation. Like Daniel Older, you might practice a bit of self-forgiveness. When a critic of your writing appears in your consciousness, walk that false critic to the home. Five minutes of this mental clearing will seem long at first.

When your five-minute timer goes off, pick up this book and go to the first exercise, at the end of Chapter 3. Read the instructions. Close and remove this book from the desk. Write a couple of notes about the exercise at the top of a fresh page, so you don't forget what it is. Set your timer for the number of minutes specified in the exercise. Work at the exercise for that number of minutes. After those minutes, close your writing notebook. Set your timer for five minutes. Spend five timed minutes again in silence, coming out of your mental writing world. Get up, stretch, and walk around. You've written today. Check off the day. Go back to your life. Do it all again on your next writing day.

I know this process sounds extremely structured, and it is. But so is your yoga class. For some reason, people assume that since writing is a creative activity, it should happen organically, spontaneously, like the opening of a flower. To which I respond that that flower would not be opening if a huge number of extremely structured genetic and metabolic processes had not directed its birth, growth, and subsequent petal-popping achievement.

When you practice this routine every time you sit down to plan writing or to write, you will make progress rapidly because your mind will learn that it can relax and focus when you sit in the chair. It's Pavlovian. Work on the exercises three times a week. The pace will be dictated by your progress. I cannot give you an exact timeline. Generally, my students and I aim to complete the exercises from each chapter in a given week, except the research writing at the end of the book, which needs to be structured according to your deadline and work habits. When you sit down to write three times a week and work your way through all the exercises, you can reasonably expect that in eleven to fifteen weeks you will have established a writing practice.

Only after a month of three-day-a-week sessions should you begin to think about modifying the process to suit yourself. You might start writing for longer periods of time. Or you might try writing in a different place. Don't change more than one thing at a time. See how that change works for you. If your work slows, go back to the original routine until you figure out another tweak you want to try.

I learned to write by writing short timed exercises like this. These days, I often write for longer—but rarely for more than four hours at a time. After four hours, my brain is shot. Professional writers do not generally write more than four hours in a day,[13] and neither should you. I strongly suggest that you never plan to write for longer than four hours, or for fewer than thirty minutes.

These days, I can click in and write almost anywhere, given a computer and my fabulous noise-cancelling earbuds. But when I am confused or scared of a project, or if I don't think I can fit writing into my schedule, I know I can carve out forty minutes from even the most complex day, and I go back to the pen and the notebook, the lamp and the desk.

---

13 My sister Nadia, a marketing communications manager in Silicon Valley for many years, tells me that four hours of intensive writing is about the maximum you can expect from a professional writer. The rest of the day can be spent on corrections or reading email or meetings. But for thinking work: four hours.

CHAPTER TWO

The Writer's Matériel

DESIGN INSTRUCTORS REQUIRE THEIR STUDENTS TO WRITE, but they rarely have time to talk with them about the backstory—the origins of meaningful marks. By this, I don't mean your design history teacher's review of *how* we make marks—cuneiform writing, clay tablets, hieroglyphics, and papyrus and all that. I mean *why* we make them. It's so odd, when you think about it—the *why* of writing. So, let's look at that now, since making meaningful marks is so much of what designers do.

MAKING MARKS

Though she recognizes signs, like the sound of kibble being poured into her bowl, my dog does not mark them down or store them. Elephants and whales, both of which use complex communication systems, aren't able to store their ideas either. Their communications are partially intuitive and partially taught by the mother to the pup—and must be intuited or taught mother-to-pup in every generation. The thoughts of the individuals of these species die with them.

On our planet, only humans have mastered the storing of long, complex, and abstract thoughts by using signs and symbols. If you watch a child pick up a stick and draw in the sand and hear the mother say, "That's an *S*," you're watching these two participate in the long history of the human drive to make marks, infuse them with meaning, and store them for later use. That drive, and the huge pile of knowledge we have built up because of it, has propelled our species' success far, far beyond that of any other species. (We've been so successful that now we're grappling with the major crises our success has created.)

Humans make marks and save them, and that making and saving is bounded by our social upbringing and culture. Ursula K. Le Guin once said that the unread story is not a story, "it is little black marks on wood pulp. The reader, reading it, makes it live: a live thing, a story."[14] Everyone who can make the culture's marks has the key to that story, to the culture's store of knowledge, and the tools for adding to that store.

The history of human ascendency is short when you compare it to other earthly timetables, and there have been some whopper stumbles and huge losses of accreted knowledge along the way. When the Roman Empire—a complex culture not unlike our own—slowly fell apart, an enormous amount of knowledge was lost with it. After the various Vandal successes and the passing of a few hundred years, most people in Europe had lost the knowledge of how to read or write Latin, the language of Rome, and it died. (Later, when the first universities were created, Latin was revived as the language of the intellect. But everyday people never spoke it again.) When people cannot decode the signs of their culture, they have no access to its store of knowledge and they cannot rise in the social order. Human mark-making is the key to accreted wisdom, and accreted wisdom makes civilization possible.

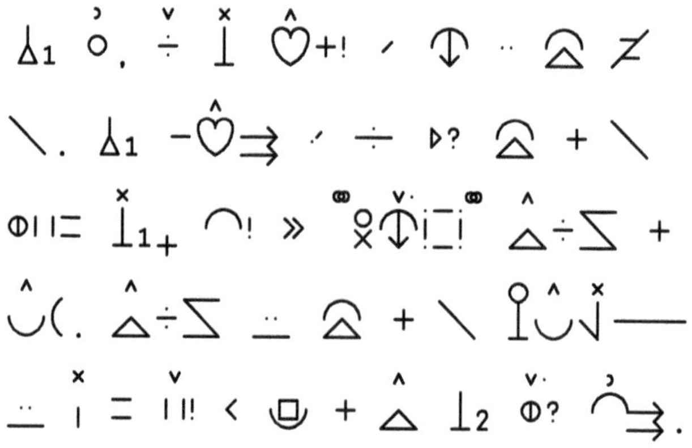

MARKS INTO SIGNS

fig 2.1

Ideographic and pictographic "Blissymbols."

As I've mentioned, some people like the idea that design is one thing and writing something else. But I take issue with that division because design and writing are variants of our human talent for systemized mark-making and preservation. Mark-making is where design and writing hold hands—where they're closer in content and manufacture than you may have been led to believe.

---

14 Ursula K. Le Guin, *Dancing at the Edge of the World: Thoughts on Words, Women, Places* (New York: Grove Press, 1992), 198.

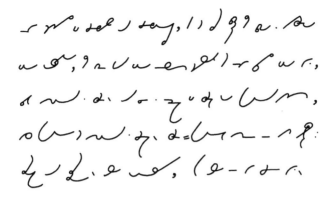

Signs into Sign Bundles

In the study of semiotics and semiology—which is very useful if you're a designer or writer—if one sound or mark stands for another idea or thing, it's called a *sign*. And when a number of signs are bundled together, that bundle is called a *symbol*.[15] Sign-bundles come in two types: verbal and visual. They're related, but they're not the same thing.

Verbal sign-bundles are made from the various sounds that humans make. Visual sign-bundles are made from things that are drawn, photographed, stitched, tattooed—any mode of utterance made from materials outside the human vocal apparatus. As we have just seen, the sign-bundles humans make have a shelf life of thousands of years, if someone is around to read them, and can be decoded by someone living long, long after their makers are dust—if the symbol system of the culture has not been lost.

Bill Hill, the inventor of Microsoft's TrueType, suggested that reading began earlier than all this symbol making, because people learned to "read" tracking signs in the wild, interpreting the shapes of footprints and broken twigs left by wild animals. He believed that early hunters first followed these signs, then began making their own piles of stones or twig-shapes or imprints to let their companions know what was going on, that game was near—the warthog had gone that-a-way—that they were following that doomed warthog. Hill

fig 2.2

Shorthand stenographic script is loosely phonetic.

---

15 We are using terms that are found in the study of signs and symbols called semiotics. Semiotics is a branch of the study of logic, and it provides useful terms. The study of language that closely resembles semiotics is called semiology, and was first thought out by Ferdinand Saussure, a linguist. Designers tend to favor semiotics over semiology because its original inventor, the strange and wonderful Charles Peirce, was interested in the way *images* worked. People often mash semiotics and semiology together because they have many overlapping ideas and seek to describe many of the same things, but they come from different places and are concerned about different things.

believed that following tracks led to organizing these bits and pieces of bark and twig into signs that had meanings for the next hunter, and that really was the invention of reading. If we embrace his theory, then we can say that "reading" was invented before writing—and way before alphabets or spelled-out words or phrases were invented.[16]

ˈlɛtərz ɑr saɪnz ðæt dɪˈskraɪb ˈvɜrbəl saʊndz, bʌt ðæts ˈoʊnli pɑrt ʌv wʌt ðeɪ du. æz ju meɪ rɪˈmɛmbər frʌm dɪˈzaɪn ˈhɪstəri, itʃ ˈlɛtər hæz ɪts oʊn hɪˈstɔrɪkəl ˈminɪŋ dəˈraɪvd frʌm "mɑrk fɔr ə haʊs" ɔr eɪ "hɛd ʌv ə ʃip," ɔr ˌwʌˈtɛvər ði əˈrɪdʒənəl ˈmɛtəfɔr wʌz ðæt fɜrst ˈprɑmptəd ðə səgˈnɪfɪkənt mɑrk. soʊ, ə wɪsp ʌv ˈminɪŋ frʌm ɪts ˈhɪstəri ɪz ˈkærid əˈlɔŋ wɪð ɪts ˈlɑrdʒər ˈfʌŋkʃən ʌv dɪˈskraɪbɪŋ ðoʊz saʊndz. ðɛn itʃ ˈlɛtər goʊz ɑn tu wɜrk wɪˈðɪn ðə sɪˈstɛmɪk ˈstrʌktʃər ʌv ən ˈælfəˌbɛt.

BUNDLING BUNDLES

fig 2.3

International Phonetic Alphabet (IPA).

Letters are signs that describe verbal sounds, but that's only part of what they do. As you may remember from design history, each letter has its own historical meaning derived from "mark for a house" or a "head of a sheep," or whatever the original metaphor was that first prompted the significant mark. So, a wisp of meaning from its history is carried along with its larger function of describing those sounds. Then each letter goes on to work within the systemic structure of an alphabet.

ALPHABETS ARE SYSTEMS

Alphabets are refined systems of signs, or characters.[17] You learned your "alphabet" when still a lisping infant, using music to tie these unrelated signs into relationship.

In English, one of the first things children learn is that "A" always comes before "B" and never after "C." This alphabetic system stands on its own as a system of grouping unrelated to words, and we use it mostly as a technique for storing

---

16 I enjoyed interviewing Bill Hill about his ideas on reading and reading-on-screen. Natalia Ilyin. "Tracking Bill Hill," accessed September 18, 2017, http://www.commarts.com/column/tracking-bill-hill.

17 Alphabetic writing can be traced to the consonantal writing system used by Semitic languages in the Levant in the 2nd millennium BCE. According to Sampson, nearly all alphabetic scripts used today can be traced to this Semitic proto-alphabet. Geoffrey Sampson, *Writing Systems: A Linguistic Introduction* (Redwood City: Stanford University Press, 1985) 77.

information. The alphabet is the "first sorting" of letterforms into a separate system of meaning. And then the words begin.

Language uses the same parts of your brain that playing a game uses. Language has rules. You learn the rules to play the game. When you form a word in a language, you're allowed only to use letters from that language's alphabet. If you write something in English, you don't invent your own letters. English has a particular number of letters. It's a closed system: You have no other choices. Every writer must use the same system to get thoughts on the page.

If you suddenly throw in a Ж character from the Russian alphabet, average people will think you made a mistake and designers will think you're trying to look like Rodchenko. If you decide to invent your own meaningful character and introduce it into the system, people might start referring to you as the "Designer Formerly Known as Joe," because your new letter doesn't fit into the game. It's an unreadable disruption.

These rules constrict what you can say with language, and affect what you *think* as well as what you write. The alphabets and grammatical structures of various cultures alter the ways people can express themselves in those cultures. The very essence of what you can write in your culture is altered by the constraints of your written language.

Вот почему умение говорить и писать на другом языке делает ваши мысли и тексты глубже. Ваш мозг получает возможность обрабатывать идеи, используя две различные сложные знаковые системы, и их пересечение позволяет вам приходить к мыслям, к которым кто-то, думающий только на одном языке, не имел бы возможности прийти.

This is why speaking and writing a second language deepens your thinking and writing. Your mind gets the opportunity to process ideas using two different complex signifying systems, and the overlap allows you to consider ideas someone thinking in only one language may not have the opportunity to imagine.

fig 2.4

Cyrillic glyphs, in Russian.

Type designers spend years learning to design typefaces—a complex form of system design in which all the alphabets and numerals and extra characters—and then different weights—must all be able to work beautifully with each other. Tobias Frere-Jones once said that the best designers "are ultimately driven by a respect for—but not a slavish attachment to—history and the content of words,"[18] because the history and use of typographic forms give the letters of alphabets whole added layers of meaning.

When you set something in Comic Sans[19], you can be sure your designer friends will be disgusted (unless, of course, you do it "ironically.") Why is that? Because the layer of meaning that Comic Sans introduces to the message—the "super-sign" that Comic Sans has become—is one of false warmth and office birthday party announcements. But if you set something in, say, the typeface Exchange, no one will quite know what meanings it is introducing into your message because it is so new, and you'll have a high old time with your type friends, trying to figure out how its extracts and remixes of concepts from type history affect the words set in it.

CODING AND DECODING

You're decoding right now. Nose to the ground, you're interpreting marks and recognizing them as meaningful. When you see the letter-bundles on this page, you hear sounds in your mind, and you remember what those sounds represent to you. You see the letter-bundles, and you recognize the letter-bundles around it. The writer (me) has organized these letter-bundles into meaningful sets (we hope), according to the system of syntax that you know because your culture imposes it. That's what words and phrases and clauses and sentences are: They're societally-approved organized bundles of words, which are bundles of letters, which are bundles of graphemes, which broadly denote the phonemes of our spoken language.

Since layers of human experience are embedded in written letters and then in alphabets and then in type design and then in designing with type and, finally, in words on the screen or on the page, being truly present when manipulating these powerful little bundles of signification seems the right course of action.

---

18 http://elupton.com/2010/07/frere-jones-tobias/ [Accessed October 20, 2017].

19 Poor Vincent Connare, the designer who created Comic Sans, created it for the utterances of a comic dog named Rover, and never expected that it would become so popular, or that it would be the butt of so many designer-jokes.

CHAPTER THREE

Words

Fᴿᴼᴹ ʟᴇᴛᴛᴇʀs, ʟᴇᴛ's ɢᴏ ᴛᴏ ᴡᴏʀᴅs. Words are the most basic form of your writing practice, and word choice is the most important decision-making in your writing. You can be grammatically correct, have brilliant ideas, and scroll them all out in fine fashion, but if your words are all jargon and cliché, your good ideas are not going to have their moment with your readers. Your readers will start with excitement, but their eyes will soon glaze over, thoughts of a nap will come upon them, and the book will drop from their hands. Of all of the things you want to achieve as a writer, the most important is *to keep your reader reading*. And the way you do that is by being intelligent about choosing your words.

In the last two sections of this book, I cover some tips about which particular words *not* to use, because they are horrible clichés or impossibly pompous. But for now, here's a rule of thumb: No matter what you're writing, whether a formal piece or an informal piece (we'll get to what those are very soon) the most important thing is that you use words that *sound like you*. They should be as clean, simple, and clear as those you use when ordering your morning coffee. Even if the topic is complex, you owe it to your reader to make things as simple and direct as possible.

I'll say it again: Your words need to sound like you. They might sound like you wearing your intellectual glasses, or sound like you in flip flops, but no matter what tone, you need to pick words that you might use when speaking. Even if, as I do, you sometimes use the words associated with a particular expertise—like plumbing, say, or semiotics—the words around those words must sound like you. You don't need to rein in your vocabulary—but don't use words that you think you *should* be using. Don't start using academic jargon if you can at all help it. If you wouldn't say it to your intelligent neighbor, don't say it in your thesis.

People who feel that to sound educated they need to sound complex are people who are insecure—or who are afraid that their ideas cannot stand on their own. I still believe, for instance, that much of the later writing on semiotics that I read in graduate school was written solely to prove that the writers deserved tenure. But that writing confused people and kept everyday people from understanding theories that actually have value outside the ivory tower. Much academic-speak is a smokescreen for insecurity—for what shall we do if normal people get these useful ideas? Where will our closely-held expertise be, then? Remember: Education is not witchcraft, and hocus-pocus has no place in the academy.

Sometimes a well-meaning person will give you a lecture about words being "the building blocks of language," but I don't think that's really accurate. Words aren't blocks. They're more spongy and shape-shifting than blocks. Words are spongy little mirrors. (Hmmm ... perhaps not the most appealing metaphor. But now I'm committed.) They mirror you and they mirror the culture in which you're writing. They soak up all kinds of prejudices and thoughts and questions and hatreds and worries from our human past.[20] They're amorphous and kinetic and annoying and constantly changing, and the things they mean and the ways they fit together are never static. If you don't believe this, try using the word "niggardly" in conversation.[21]

Even in the most skilled writer's hands, the message sent by these bundles and the message received from them are *not the same message*. When you read this, the thought in your mind is not the same one I am trying to "get across" to you. Your idea of the meanings of the words you're reading is influenced by everything that surrounds them in your mind—all your experiences, all the cultural influences they passed through as they moved from me to you.

In my beloved semiotics,[22] that new idea-in-your-mind is called the

---

20 I've known certain extremely thoughtful students who worry that the entire language is corrupted and that they will never be able to use it to get their ideas across cleanly. But think of writing in design terms: Every type style you use is embedded with meaning. Every image you choose is imbued with the culture of your era. Does this keep you from making design? Musicians must include their instrument's shortcomings as a condition of the music. Rather than ignoring those shortcomings, or wishing them away, or not playing the instrument, they accept its limits and work with them—introduce them into the playing. As writers, we must accept the limits of language, and write; as designers, we must accept the limits of image and type—or else share the fate of the elephant and the orca.

21 "Niggardly" is an adjective meaning "stingy" or "miserly." It comes from the Middle English word *nigon*, which means the same thing, and may be related to the Old Norse verb *nigla*, which means "to fuss about small matters." This very old word, from around 1066, has no relationship etymologically to the similar-sounding racial slur. That slur traces its roots back to the Spanish and Portuguese word "negro," meaning "black" which traders used to describe the Bantu peoples they enslaved around 1442. The word "niggardly" never meant anything racial. But because it sounds so much like the slur, it has gained meaning from the slur. These days, we don't want others to mistake the word we are using, and so we never use the word "niggardly." Through no fault of its own, the word will disappear in our lifetimes. This is an example of semiotic "interpretant"—the new sign-in-the-mind grabs ideas from our context and incorporates them, reflecting our own times and prejudices.

22 Semiotics is interesting to me because it provides a structure with which to examine what designers make and the ways these objects *mean*.

"interpretant."[23] This, although a large word, is a very useful word, valuable because there's no other word that means what it means. The interpretant is the new sign that is created in the mind of the receiver of a sign. When someone bats a sign over to you, what settles in your brain is a different sign all together from the original one batted. As a writer and designer—and human—you're playing this badminton game of sign-transfer all the time.

We could say that all human communication is really an extended game of "telephone"—that old parlor game in which you say something in the ear of the person sitting next to you and that person repeats it to the next person, and so on, and by the time it gets around the circle to you again it's a totally different sentence. In the language of semiotics, that is the game of communication, and is called "endless semiosis."

It's amazing that we ever get any ideas across at all with our written and spoken efforts, with our videos and motion pieces and VR. When you think of some of the abstruse ideas humans do actually communicate to each other, it borders on the miraculous that we've managed as well as we have. Thank heavens for the narrower interpretant inherent in the signifiers of mathematics and science, or we would have blown ourselves up years ago.

"When you have mastered numbers," W. E. B. Du Bois said, "you will in fact no longer be reading numbers, any more than you read words when reading books. You will be reading meanings."

We speak words and write words, but they never quite mean what we are trying to mean. People have always craved being completely understood, but all visual and verbal communication, even at its very finest, is approximate. Perhaps our inability to communicate completely through signs is at the center of our uniquely human sense of isolation from the workings of nature and the cosmos. Perhaps this is why music and falling in love and some kinds of spiritual experiences are so deeply satisfying. They give us the sense of true communication—of being completely understood.

DENOTATION AND CONNOTATION

The definition of a word is what it *denotes*. The meanings that attach themselves to that definition are what the word *connotes*. For instance, the word "white"

---

23 "Interpretant" is a very useful term for designers. It comes from Charles Sanders Peirce's "triadic" theory of the sign. If you like this sort of thing, you might read Steven Skaggs excellent book, *Fire Signs: A Semiotic Theory for Graphic Design*. MIT Press, 2017.

denotes a color, but one of its connotations is racial. If you write well, you're able to use words in ways that make decoding as clean and clear as possible, while manipulating their *denotation* and *connotation* to produce a desired outcome in the mind of the reader.

Sending and receiving signs—also known as writing or designing—is a two-way street. The way a piece is written or designed will depend on the writer's age, social background, socioeconomic status, values, upbringing, and influences. Those aspects of the maker's world and mindset can be read in the text or the made object. So, while you're reading the ideas, you're also picking up much about the writer. And when you see the design, you learn much about the designer.

Try to use words that reflect the identity and values you choose, those most authentic to you and at the same time most invisible to others. Why invisible? So that people do not find themselves tripping over your usage, tone, or style, and have the opportunity to focus on your ideas. You make thousands of choices when you're writing, all to make the medium conform to your being, your beliefs, and your values.

Some writers like the feeling of using the exactly right word with the exactly right meaning at exactly the right time. These people tend to write prose. Some writers use a word because they like the way it feels to say it, what it conjures in the mind. These people tend to write poetry. But before you think you must choose between writing prose and poetry, remember not all prose writing must be the most direct means to an end. Great prose has poetry in it.[24] Cadence and flow are just as important in an academic paper as they are in a poem. Academics forget that. I am here to remind you. You're still a serious prose writer if you let the poetry in.

Focusing In

I suggest that, as you begin writing, you focus your attention on the words you use in your everyday speech. If you listen to the words you use when you speak, you'll start to write better. The best writing flows like spoken language—cleaned-up spoken language. Try speaking into a voice-recorder. Talk about anything you care about. Then play it back and listen to the ways you put words together.

---

24 To prove this to yourself, read "Letter 4" in Rainer Maria Rilke's *Letters to a Young Poet*, published in 1929, which is something that you will be glad you read. "Perhaps you do carry within you the possibility of creating and forming, as an especially blessed and pure way of living; train yourself for that but take whatever comes, with great trust, and as long as it comes out of your will, out of some need of your innermost self, then take it upon yourself, and don't hate anything."

 **per·son** (pûr´sən) *n.*

An individual capable of independent thought and action.

— **hu·man** (hyōō´mən) *n.*

A member of the species *Homo-sapiens*. Different from other apes because of its large brain, opposable thumbs, ability to speak, and making and decoding of symbols.

— **bod·y** (bŏd´ē) *n.*

The entire physical structure of a living thing, and of large objects like cars and texts.

— **soul** (sōl) *n.*

In the dualist view, the center of the human being's conscience, morality, and appreciation of art and music.

fig 3.1

The denotation *of the idea of a "person" is a clear representation of* Homo-sapiens. *But the* connotations *of the idea of a "person" are numerous. Are you building an argument about how design can support the self-actualized life of a* human being? *Are you writing a paper on* mortality? *On the ways design can make death less scary? Does your piece center on the notion of design's impact on* individual *identity? Or on how designers teach people to view their* corporeal bodies *in culturally-confined ways? Are you discussing the ways design can reflect the striving of the* soul? *All of these are aspects of human life: All are* connotations *of the word, "person."*

How many of your words did you actually choose for yourself? How many were terms you've picked up from social media? How much was you? How much was bombast and filler?

I use speech-recognition on my phone sometimes when an idea hits me during my commute on the ferry. The first time I used the app, I was excited about an idea and recorded it in what felt like a terse and businesslike fashion. Later that evening I read the transcript. Long spates of educator-jargon. Clichés. Sudden tangents. Many an "um," "ah," "really," "like," and "actually." Demented periods of humming.

I couldn't believe how poorly I spoke: I wondered how my students are ever able to take cogent notes in my classes. The second time I used the recorder, I concentrated on my argument, on being convincing. The transcript came a lot closer to a written first draft and I felt a lot better about my brain. Recording is not a replacement for an actual written draft, but it will give you written material to start moving around on the page, will kick start you if you're blocking, and is a great hurdle jump if you're dyslexic.

EXERCISE ONE
Seven Beautiful Words

Start with your five-minute focusing exercise from the first chapter.

Then spend thirty minutes making a list of the seven words that you think are the most beautiful in the English language. Spend thirty minutes, not two minutes. It's hard to stay focused, but you can do it. Think of beauty. What does it mean to you? What words come up when you think of experiences you deem "beautiful"? Stick with your experiences. They're your compass.

When beginning the exercise, ask yourself:

— Which words make me feel happy just to say them?
— What first comes to my mind when I think of the word "joy?"

After initial resistance to such a "simple" task, your brain-chatter will calm down and you will find seven beautiful words and list them in your notebook. Don't forget to do your five minutes of meditation coming out of your writing.

CHAPTER FOUR

Phrase to Clause to Sentence

T HIS IS NOT A GRAMMAR BOOK, and we aren't going to go deeply into the whole system and structure of English, its morphology, inflections, or phonology—which I am betting you never learned because I certainly never did until I was in my thirties—but we do need to talk briefly about how sentences are formed in English.[25]

---

25 I was never taught serious grammar until I took Latin in college, at which point I was introduced to diagramming sentences, fell madly in love with this physical charting process, and could yak about objective complements and adverbial clauses till the cows came home. If no one taught you this bit of arcane fun in "Language Arts," and if you are the kind of person who loves a visual system, I suggest you play around with diagramming sentences in order to learn everything about grammar. I recommend *Grammar by Diagram: Understanding English Grammar Through Traditional Sentence Diagramming*, Cindy L. Vitto. ISBN-13: 978-1551114576.

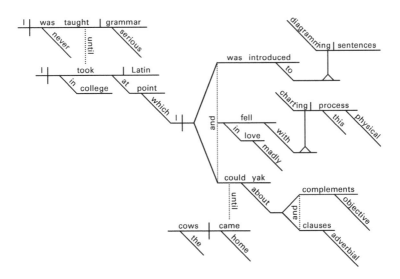

If you're dyslexic or have trouble reading, get someone to read this chapter to you while you lie on your back and watch clouds. This is the only section that has a lot of grammar in it, and you need to hear and visualize the terms. After this chapter, things become a lot more about sketching and patterning and a lot less about grammar.

Syntax is an ordering system for the game of arranging words and phrases to make good sentences. Phrases bundle words, then clauses bundle phrases, then sentences bundle clauses, then paragraphs bundle sentences, then sections bundle paragraphs, then papers or articles or chapters bundle sections, then books or periodicals or web pages bundle those papers or articles or chapters. This book should really be called *Ways With Bundles*, but I'm pretty sure my editor won't go for that.

If you're like most of my students, you bundle words very well every time you speak to a barista, but you bundle them less well when you write, partially because you aren't engaging in extensive communication with said barista, and partially because your relative inexperience with writing causes you to get nervous and stilted when you put words down on paper. This is normal for designers. In order to be a good writer, you need to be comfortable with the syntax of English, and I wouldn't be putting a quick review of the basics in here for you if I thought you were comfortable with them already.

After reading a huge pile of student work over a lifetime of teaching, I'm here to tell you that stringing words together that "sound right" will only take you so far. Understanding the mechanics of how sentences go together will give you confidence in your ability to organize writing in ways that will keep your reader from nodding off to sleep. Instead of vaguely stuffing words into intervals between capitals and periods, hoping your ideas will all somehow come together in the end, imagine weighing your options, choosing among alternatives, then consciously using the right words in the right order with the right emphasis and right cadence for your purpose. James Baldwin used to say that the goal in writing is to strip yourself of all your disguises and create sentences "as clean as a bone." Both of these goals are impossibly difficult and you will spend your life working toward them.

Much of writing is the stringing together of good words to make good sentences, and then it's the logical and rhythmic ordering of those sentences. After all, before writing, people memorized long tracts of rhyme in order to pass on their history and myths. That need for internal rhyme—for music, really—remains in us. We want writing to give us the satisfaction that music gives us. Syntax and word order reinforce the music of your writing. Just review the next few terms and examples. When you read them over a few times, you'll remember what they mean when I start referring to them later in the book.[26]

Knowing basic syntactic terms makes life easier when you're a writer because it's the jargon of the craft, and your editors will use it. You don't have to have this writing knowledge to put things down on paper, but then you don't have to know anything about the principles of graphic design to use InDesign, either. And we all know how that turns out. Pardon me while I drop this shadow.

First, the stuff I am not going to review. I am expecting that you know what a *noun* is, what a *verb* is, what an *adjective* is, and what an *adverb* is. I am expecting that you know what a *preposition* is, a *conjunction* is, and an *article* is. If you do not know these things, please Google them. I am also expecting that you know to capitalize sentences and how to end them with a period. These are my full expectations of you.

FIRST, PHRASES

When grammarians put words in bundles, the first bundle they create is the *phrase*. These are small groups of words that form a meaningful unit, usually within a *clause*, which we're going to get to in a second. Web crawlers look for common words and phrases because phrases are the simplest of word constructions, and they are the most easily recognized.

— A *noun phrase* is built around a single noun:

> A tiny green *frog* sat on my thumbnail.
> He was reading a *book* about puff pastry.

— A *verb phrase* is the verbal part of a clause:

> She had been *designing* large scuffs.
> But now she will be *writing* a very small zine.

---

26 Although I wrote a book about how Modernism has driven me crazy, I am a modernist writer. (There's irony for you.) Like modernist designers, modernist writers focus on stripping away extras. They want to get at the cleanest way to transmit their thoughts. Some writers don't believe that writing should aim for clarity, but in my world, and in our profession, clarity is key. I read for a simple reason: to learn how other people have negotiated life—and I think most people read for that reason.

— An *adjectival phrase* is—fairly obviously—built around an adjective:

> He heard a very *appealing* bird.
>
> This bird was *large*, yet fluttery.

— And, last but not least, an *adverbial phrase* is built around an adverb:

> She sneaked up on him very *quietly*.
>
> And took the donut as *fast* as possible.

Phrases are the real powerhouses of a sentence. If you run across the phrase, "nice day," you don't spend a lot of time wondering about it. You've seen that phrase hundreds of times, and you recognize it in the same way that you would recognize a single word. But the phrase "summer afternoon" is a different story: You don't see the phrase "summer afternoon" very often, so your mind imbues it with its own memories and images, makes its own *interpretant*, and the effect of the phrase becomes much more intense.[27]

NOW, CLAUSES

From phrases, it's just a hop to clauses.[28] Clauses use phrases, but they are at the next level of complexity. They have a *subject* and a *predicate*. Basically, a *subject* is the thing that you're talking about, a *predicate* is the thing that is happening around or with or to the thing you're talking about. I'll discuss predicates again in a bit, so don't get overwhelmed if all this is starting to whirl around in your head.

If you look at the clause, "When the professor spoke," you can see that "professor" is the subject, and "spoke" is the predicate. But that "when" makes the clause not quite a sentence. It's not complete in itself: It's leaning toward another clause to complete it. It is a *dependent clause*.

---

27 Henry James is famously known for saying that he thought the most beautiful phrase in the English language was "summer afternoon." What did those two words summon up for him? We don't know. We only know what his words summon up for us, and that's why they're so evocative.

28 "Clause" comes from the Latin word, *claudere*, which means "closed." These little bundles are closed thoughts, instead of being open-ended, in the way phrases are.

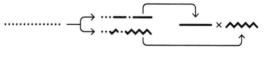

1
OPEN PHRASE

2
**DIFFERENTIATION
INTO SUBJECT/PREDICATE**

3
**FORMATION OF
A CLAUSE BUNDLE**

But if you look at the clause, "they drifted off to sleep," you can see that "they" is the subject, and "drifted off to sleep" is the predicate. It is a little sentence. It's an *independent clause*.

So, a clause that can stand on its own is an *independent* clause, and one that needs something to shore it up is called a *dependent* clause.

"When the professor spoke, they drifted off to sleep," is a *complex* or *compound* sentence because it consists of more than one clause, a dependent clause and an independent clause. I include this grammatical tidbit so that the next time you're in my office and I say, "There's a problem here with your predicate—you're trying to make a sentence out of two dependent clauses," you won't look at me like the round-eyed emoji.

EXERCISE TWO

Seven Beautiful Clauses

We're going to add some time to this exercise: Write 5-50-5, or five minutes in, fifty minutes writing, five minutes out.

Start with your five-minute focusing exercise.

Make seven phrases, at least one for each kind of phrase—a noun phrase, a verb phrase, an adjectival phrase, and an adverbial phrase. Use your seven beautiful words liberally, making phrases that sound like parts of poems or words in a song.

Then make your phrases into seven clauses. What must you do to turn a phrase into a clause?

Spend a full fifty minutes on these phrases and clauses.

List them in your notebook.

Don't forget to spend five minutes coming out of your writing.

FINALLY, SENTENCES

Short sentences, like short letters, can be harder to write than long ones. (I'm assuming you're not James Joyce and have not spent years learning to compose a sentence that takes up a full page.) If you're like many designers, you tend to add on to sentences as you go, starting at one end and wandering around till you think you may want to end it. We, the *Committee for Design Writing Improvement*, would like you to stop this wandering immediately. Wandering is something we want you to do in a dusky Irish wood in the wake of a glimmering sprite, not in a sentence that we're going to be called upon to read.

Stop the Wandering

In other areas of your life, you can leap, expecting the net to appear, but not in a sentence. So, before you start to write, know two things. First: What are you writing about? Again, that's the *subject* of your sentence. Don't start writing and ramble along, clearing your throat and mumbling, waiting for the subject to appear. Know the subject of your sentence before you start to write. Second: What are you saying about your subject? What is it doing or what is it like? That's the *predicate* of your sentence.[29] It's the information that completes your idea about the subject.

Because we, the *Committee for Design Writing Improvement*,[30] want this book to be more than just cheery words of encouragement and praise, I am now going to list a bunch of examples of kinds of *predicates*, providing a bit of grammatical meat into which I recommend you sink your teeth.

   Andrea *designs*.
— This is a "verb-only predicate."

   Jared *chomps leaves*.
— This is a "verb + direct object predicate."

   Anna's son, Wes, *silkscreened a toaster*.
— This is a "verb + indirect object + direct object predicate."

   Jeff *talked to the semiaquatic rodent*.
— This is a "verb + prepositional object predicate."

   Jacob *named her dictator*.
— This is a "verb + object + predicative noun predicate."

---

29 Grammarians use two different definitions of the term "predicate." We are using the traditional one. There's another one that's fairly abstruse, derived from "predicate logic," and you can get into that after you've mastered this, but there's no real need for you to ever look under that rock unless so inclined.

30 One of my students assumed this Committee to be a real thing and wondered how she could get in touch with it to offer design services, since it didn't seem to have a website. I felt sheepish telling her it is not a real thing: It is I.

> Tiffany *serenaded him on the subway.*

— This is a "verb + object + adjunct predicate."

> Susan *pranced in the fountain.*

— This is a "verb + predicative prepositional phrase predicate."

Three Sentence Writers

Okay! Enough. I just want you to know that this information exists, and that building sentences is a well-studied and documented practice. Since you're now aware of this fact, in the next exercise we will pattern and design sentences. But first I want to mention three people who are known for their excellent sentences. They're Samuel Johnson, Virginia Woolf, and Louis Sullivan, and you can learn from all of them.

I'll start with Samuel Johnson. He is one of my favorite people of all time, and if I were stuck on a desert island it would be him with whom I would desire to be stuck. Dr. Johnson lived in London in the 1700s, so this is going back a bit. He had to leave Oxford because he didn't have the money to keep going, and while his friends were getting their prestigious degrees he was scurrying around London writing hackwork and living in a garret. But during that time, he read everything that was available as a book or manuscript in the London of the time. Everything. (In those days, it was actually possible for a person to read most of what had been published. Owning 120 books was considered a robust library.) So, Samuel Johnson scraped together a living in London and published a number of articles. After years of barely making it financially (but gaining an increasing reputation for genius and scholarship), he got a contract to write a huge project: the first comprehensive English dictionary. (The French had an entire *académie* of forty people write their dictionary. But the English asked one man—Samuel Johnson.)

Sometime after this project was long over, the king gave him a pension, so he didn't starve to death. And Oxford gave him an honorary degree, which was thoughtful. He had a huge brain and huge knowledge. He had bad bouts of depression, feared things and loved things, and let people live in his house who had nowhere else to go. He was extremely human and messed up and also kind and brilliant. And he wrote some amazing sentences.

During the dictionary project, long after he'd spent the advance, to keep his creditors from putting him in debtor's prison, he dashed off short essays—often while the printer's messenger waited at the door for his manuscript. His facility with sentence structure allowed him to write very fast and very well under extreme circumstances. Here's a paragraph you might appreciate, the end of an essay he wrote about procrastination—something he fought all his life:

> The certainty that life cannot be long, and the probability that it will be much shorter than nature allows, ought to awaken every man to the active prosecution of whatever he is desirous to perform. It is true that no diligence can ascertain success; death may intercept the swiftest career; but he who is cut off in the execution of an honest undertaking, has at least the honour of falling in his rank, and has fought the battle, though he missed the victory.[31]

This paragraph is two sentences long. When you read the sentences again, looking for the clauses, you'll notice how the urgency of the sentences builds. In the first sentence, he states a fact, modifies that fact, then states a supposition. In the second sentence, he states a fact, modifies that fact—and then whomps us with the rolling thunder of the conclusion: statement, statement, statement: bittersweet punch. It's like a Muhammad Ali knockout.

Virginia Woolf once said that writing is "putting words on the backs of rhythms."[32] She believed that most of the hard work of writing is in composing the music of the phrases, clauses, and sentences. This is one of the sentences from her novel, *To the Lighthouse*:

> Not liking to think of him so, and wondering if they had guessed at dinner why he suddenly became irritable when they talked about fame and books lasting, wondering if the children were laughing at that, she twitched the stocking out, and all the fine gravings came drawn with steel instruments about her lips and forehead, and she grew still like a tree which has been tossing and quivering and now, when the breeze falls, settles, leaf by leaf, into quiet.[33]

---

31 Don't let past writers' use of the masculine pronoun irritate you. Up until just a few years ago, people were taught that the male pronoun was inclusive, and for that reason writers used it to mean everyone. Of course, now all that has changed. However, this change has caused a grave temptation. It's tempting to alter the prose of former writers to make their pronouns current. Alert: Don't "update" anything written by someone else. When I see that some well-meaning person has changed out the pronouns in a famous piece of writing so as to make it more palatable to the current sensibility, I want to wring that person's neck. That's historical revisionism, it messes with the original, it's not honest, it keeps us from reading what was really there, and it's a rotten thing to do to another person's writing, whether they're dead or not. Do you want someone editing your words without your consent? I didn't think so. *Johnson: Rambler #134 (June 29, 1751)*.

32 "All writing is nothing but putting words on the backs of rhythm. If they fall off the rhythm one's done." Letter to Ethel Smyth, April 1931. And, now that we seem to be quoting Woolf: "Style is a very simple matter; it is all rhythm. Once you get that, you can't use the wrong words. But on the other hand here am I sitting after half the morning, crammed with ideas, and visions, and so on, and can't dislodge them, for lack of the right rhythm." Letter to Vita Sackville-West, March 1926.

33 Virginia Woolf. *To the Lighthouse* (London: Hogarth Press, 1927).

Words on the backs of rhythms. Read Woolf's sentence aloud, if you would. Watch how you pause for breath. Listen for the cadence. People have thought a lot about how Woolf made her sentences. This is how Rick Barot, a Woolf scholar, deconstructs that sentence:

> There are three dependent clauses before the subject shows up; after the subject clause, the clause that some would call the fundament, three subsequent clauses appear, further modifying the subject. The three dependent clauses are all mental activities: "Not liking," "and wondering," "wondering." The latter three clauses are all physically grounded: "the fine gravings came drawn ... about her lips," "she grew still," "and now ... settles." The first three clauses are organized as participles: "liking," "wondering," and "wondering." The last three clauses are organized by that workhorse conjunction "and": "and all," "and she grew," "and now." Which is to say that on either side of the fundament, the sentence is as organized as it is intricate.[34]

People take apart her sentences because they are so complex, yet read so well. Beginning writers often assume that there's an editorial prejudice against this kind of long sentence these days. I've never encountered this prejudice in living editors, but I know that Microsoft's grammar checker will start underlining my sentences if it deems them too long. Fighting an automated grammar-checker drives me wild. Turn that thing off and use your ears. Listen to your sentences.

Perhaps, if there is a prejudice against long sentences, it's because most people don't know how to build their writing's dynamic range, so when their thoughts get long, they're most likely run-on sentences: boring, trailing-off-to-nothing, badly composed buckets of flab. But you can learn to write long sentences well by paying attention to their music, by speaking them out loud, and by varying the ways you fit your clauses together. This will make your prose more conversational and rhythmic and less like ad copy, which relies on short sentences and fragments. Vary your sentence length. When you're writing a long article or a thesis, your reader will get tired of the blandness of medium-length sentence after medium-length sentence. Make some long and some short according to the music, or cadence, of your tone. Varying sentence length is another key to keeping your reader reading.

Here's a different kind of long sentence-building. It's from a section of Louis Sullivan's *Kindergarten Chats*, which was published in 1901.[35] Louis Sullivan isn't

---

34 A wonderful short essay on Virginia Woolf's sentence structure. http://tinhouse.com/the-art-of-the-sentence-rick-barot/ Accessed: October 15, 2017.

35 Although written by an architect, *Kindergarten Chats* was recommended to me when I was studying the elements of typography with Krzysztof Lenk, proving that design principles are not material dependent.

as well-known as his famous student, Frank Lloyd Wright. But he's actually an original American modern, and the man who coined the oft-repeated mantra, "Form follows function." That's a very short sentence. But he could write a long sentence masterfully, too.

Kindergarten Chats is a book of essays in which Sullivan rolls out his ideas about how the new modern architecture should work. This is serious critical writing. It's one of the first explications of modernist design, but it's not written in the dry way you'd expect. Sullivan is whimsical. He sets up his essay as a mock-Socratic dialogue between an airy know-it-all and his doggedly down-to-earth friend. After reading *Kindergarten Chats*, design students sometimes wonder why Sullivan took the risk of writing in a way that's quirky and strange when he was trying to get a serious point across. Shouldn't serious ideas be written in serious ways?

Well, that's a good question. I think sometimes a light tone makes serious issues accessible, and I counsel my students not to adopt a falsely high and somber tone when discussing their ideas. (I also counsel them not to be too relaxed—see "Writing Tips" at the end of this book.) Most architects of the time wrote their beliefs in a lofty way, but Sullivan knew and trusted the education of his audience and took a chance. He knew the architects of his era had received a liberal arts education, which meant, at that time, that they had been schooled in classical argument. He knew they would recognize an imitation of the Socratic method because they'd been taught that way themselves.[36]

Reading his work, you'll find huge sentences that build up to crescendos, words tumbling together like wild surf with waves pounding—he writes some of the longest clauses you'll ever see—but then he'll suddenly get very direct, using ironic, short sentences for emphasis. If you think about it, he's being metaphorical with his sentence style. He's explaining the new Modernism to Edwardians, so—form following function—he mixes a flowery, seemingly Victorian prose with a direct, modern prose to create metaphorical contrast. And, by playing around with sentence structure, he keeps his audience reading. Because he keeps them reading, they have time to integrate his ideas with their own views. Creating

---

36 The Socratic method is a way of teaching in which two people (usually a teacher and a student) argue formally. The teacher asks a question and the student answers it, then the teacher asks another question based on the student's answer, and on and on until either they go off the rails and into the weeds or some resolution is reached. I find that this technique stimulates critical thinking. It is dialectical, which means the participants defend their views and try to lead each other into contradiction. It sounds scary, but it doesn't have to be at all. If you have not been taught this way, I suggest you find a teacher or friend who will play this game with you. It hones your thinking.

sentences that give your reader enough time to focus and mull over your argument is a crucial element of writing well.

In this sentence, Sullivan's "modernist" persona explains that he's almost through with his rant about how architecture should reflect the needs of the people:

> We are rounding out our absorbing study of Democracy. Thus, turning slowly upon the momentous axis of our theme, are we coming more and more fully into the light of our sun: the refulgent and resplendent and life-giving sun of our art—an art of aspirant democracy! Let us then be on our way; for our sun is climbing ever higher. Let us be a-doing; lest it set before we know the glory and the import of its light, and we sink again into the twilight and the gloom from which we have come.[37]

Sullivan is being ironic, he uses overly flowery language to get his point across. And on that note, let us be a-doing and end this discussion of syntax. Remember to review the vocabulary at the beginning of this chapter every once in a while, so that you remember it, and as you go through this next exercise, don't hold yourself to short sentences—build musical sentences by varying the lengths of your clauses.

EXERCISE THREE
Seven Beautiful Sentences

This exercise is 5-40-5.

Begin your five-minute meditation, entering your mental writing space.

Now you will write seven beautiful sentences. You can use your seven clauses, but you don't have to. You can use your seven words as many times as you would like to make new phrases, clauses, simple sentences and then complex sentences. Review subjects and predicates and try different combinations.

Make the most beautiful sentences you can make. Make them so clear and true that if these are the only seven sentences left from all that will have been your life, they will be enough. Write them as "clean as a bone," as James Baldwin said. Spend as long as you need, but not less than forty minutes.

Exit your writing with your five-minute meditation. Moving abruptly from total mental focus to the babble of the outside world is not easy for your brain, so do try

---

37 Louis Sullivan, *Kindergarten Chats*, Ch. 36: Another City. George Wittenborn, Inc., 1918.

The certainty that
    life cannot be long,
    and the probability that
    it will be much shorter than
    nature allows,
    ought to awaken every man to
    the active prosecution of
        whatever he is desirous to perform.

It is true that
    no diligence can ascertain success;
    death may intercept the swiftest career;
    but he who is cut off in
    the execution of
    an honest undertaking,
    has at least the honour of
    falling in his rank,
    and has fought the battle,
        though he missed the victory.

Not liking to think of him so, and wondering if they had guessed at dinner why he suddenly became irritable when they talked about fame and books lasting, wondering if the children were laughing at that, she twitched the stocking out, and all the fine gravings came drawn with steel instruments about her lips and forehead, and she g-r-e-w still like a tree which has been t-o-s-s-ing and quivering and n-o-w, when the breeze falls, settles, leaf by leaf, into quiet.

We are rounding out our absorbing study of Democracy.

Thus, turning slowly upon the momentous axis of our theme, are we coming more and more fully into the light of our sun: the refulgent and resplendent and life-giving sun of our art—an art of aspirant democracy!

Let us then be on our way; for our sun is climbing ever higher.

Let us be a-doing; lest it set before we know the glory and the import of its light, and we sink again into the twilight and the gloom from which we have come.

fig 4.1

Johnson builds dynamic tension within sentences by stacking independent clauses on top of each other. We keep reading because we want to find out where he's going. Woolf composes her sentences like music: We're carried along on her rhythms and lyricism. Her sentence structure also gives us insight into how her characters think. Sullivan mixes very long and very short sentences. We're hanging on to a small boat in stormy seas, and keep reading because we're caught in the maelstrom.

to come out of writing slowly. If you're having trouble focusing and getting into the writing, don't beat yourself up. Just keep bringing your mind back to the task at hand for at least forty minutes. Then check off another session.

You might add another sentence exercise: Try using your beautiful words and phrases in a sentence that imitates the cadence, punctuation, and clause structure of one of the ones you read by Samuel Johnson, Virginia Woolf, or Louis Sullivan. The sentence doesn't need to make perfect sense—the key is to capture the feeling of each very different sentence structure.

CHAPTER FIVE

A Dash Through Punctuation

AS I MENTIONED EARLIER, I am expecting that you know that a period goes at the end of a sentence. Again, a sentence is a complete thought, containing a subject and a predicate. Most design students are pretty good at knowing when to use a period. Though sometimes they do forget that only independent clauses can stand alone. For instance, the phrase you just read is ungrammatical. (The "though" makes it a dependent clause.) Ungrammatical, but useful. Ack! Another ungrammatical "sentence"—this time with no subject. Oh no. I can't stop. That last sentence was ungrammatical too; it has no predicate. Using phrases—called fragments—as sentences is a common copywriter trick, mostly used to convey a breezy feeling in ads for soft drinks. These fragments can become a bad habit, so don't lean on them too heavily. Use them for emphasis in informal writing. And never in academic writing.

Aside from the period, the uses of punctuation are a bit vague in the minds of my students, and so we will now take a look at the options. We shall stick to the basics: a run through commas, semicolons, colons, and dashes. Do not drop into slumber. Learn this now, and you will never have to learn it again. Skim past it, and you will be hampered in your writing forevermore, trapped at a low level of play.

fig 5.1

Essential marks for writing.

Like letters and words, punctuation is a system of signs. These signs exist to help you order your thought, make it understandable to the reader, and represent the music of speech on the page. The natural rhythms of speech are called its "cadence," and particular cadences mean different things, just as different tempos of music convey different feelings.[38]

Short sentences bark. Long sentences might sound like drifts of thought, like drifts of feathers falling from punctured pillows, or like the slow breathing of a child lost in sleep; or they can hammer all into unity, sum up your argument, and put a bow on the box: It's up to you—you're the writer. When you get used to using them, commas, semicolons, colons, and dashes will direct the flow of your writing's rhythm. Varied sentence structures are the mark of a writer; they make your writing more chewy and interesting.

Punctuation has been codified over the years, and though it does change, it doesn't change nearly as fast as words and usage do.

FURTHER READING
Strunk & White

The best book I know that spells out every variable of punctuation and grammar is *The Elements of Style*, by the famed Messrs. William Strunk, Jr. and E. B. White, (the same author who wrote *Charlotte's Web*) and I suggest you buy this little book of commands and read one command a day until you have finished it.

I more than suggest it; I require it. That's why this section is called out as an exercise.[39]

---

38 Long ago I heard the idea that music is "a sign system with no fixed referents," which is a fantastic notion if you think about it: It's an entire sign-system with no common meanings attached to its signifiers. This means that everything in the language of music can mean everything. Its meaning depends entirely on the person who is playing it, and on the person who is hearing it. I may have gotten this idea indirectly from the ideas of semiotician Vladimir Karbusicky in his *Musical Signification: Essays in the Semiotic Theory and Analysis of Music*, by way of an essay by R. Hatten and G. Henrotte in *The Semiotic Web* 1987, Thomas A Sebeok, Ed., which contains a marvelous quote: "Music affects the listener by means of continuous signs of indefinite lexicality."

39 The little book by Strunk and White can seem dry to students if they read it too fast. Slower, and they catch on to the book's quiet humor. The two men who wrote the book were both very smart, quick-witted people, not boring pedants. Sit down, focus, and enjoy a tiny section at a time. After you've studied *The Elements of Style*, you really do know everything you will ever need to know about grammar and syntax. That's why the book's been in print for sixty years.

After learning how to use a period—like a car, a sentence needs brakes first—you need to be comfortable with when to use a comma. And with a discussion of the comma, I must tell you a story, lest you currently believe that punctuation isn't crucial to your world.

The story goes that Abram Andreivich Boratynski, a Russian nobleman, lived in the Tambov Province, where, in his later years, he took care of various judicial duties for the czarist government of Paul I. (This was in the early 1800s.) He generally dealt with resolving land disputes, squabbles about who owned the well—this sort of thing—but one day he got a telegram from the czar that said a political prisoner had been arrested and was in the Tambov prison, and that this unfortunate rabble-rouser should be executed.

Abram Andreivich was not in favor of executing anybody. So, he wrote a telegram back, asking if there were any way that the czar could pardon this prisoner, stating various humanitarian reasons, his execution leaving a wife and children to destitution, and so forth. The answer came back quickly: "Pardon impossible, execute."

Abram Andreivich thought a bit, then took up a penknife and pen and moved the comma, so that the message now read: "Pardon, impossible execute." He sent it along to the warden, and the warden freed the prisoner, who immediately grabbed his wife and children and set off for points unknown.[40]

All this to say—commas have power. Aside from employing them to save lives, use a comma when you:

— 1   List a series of three or more things that share a single conjunction—this is the famous serial, or Oxford, comma.

Her hair turned pink, green, and purple.

They romped, sowed their wild oats, and finally became arthritic and worn.

— 2   Enclose a parenthetical expression.

The students, who had been snoring, began to open their eyes.

George, a rodent, felt remarkably fit.

---

40   The story of Abram Andreivich's neat trick has been told and retold. Online I see he sometimes morphs into the czarina or into "a sympathetic messenger." It's a very malleable and Russian kind of story.

— 3   Introduce an independent clause that starts with a conjunction.

> There was cause for alarm, but nobody stopped eating profiteroles.
>
> She did something, and then did something else.

Some people suggest putting in a comma in every time you take a breath while reading your piece out loud. That's vague instruction, but reading out loud can alert you to the need for some sort of punctuation. The style right now is to use fewer rather than more commas, so use fewer than you're tempted to use.

Of all the punctuation my students use, they find semicolons the most confusing. It's worth de-confusing yourself. The semicolon is the unsung hero of long sentences. This is the trick to keep in mind: Using a semicolon always suggests a close relationship between the clauses that you're attaching. I find it most useful in these two situations:

— 1   Joining two independent clauses that are related in content.

> He was large; she was squashed.
>
> They took off their shoes and poured out the sand; never were two people happier.

— 2   Setting off complex descriptions in a series.

> She tried on three things: a bright yellow pair of gabardine trousers with
> tremendous patch pockets; a pair of lavender heels with embroidered grapes;
> and a small fedora covered in white rose blossoms.

If you use the semicolon in these two ways you'll be able to design longer sentences that won't give way under you just when they're starting to build to a big idea.

Using the colon is a lot simpler than using the semicolon:

— 1   Use a colon after an independent clause to introduce a list.

> Her library held three kinds of books: yellowing first editions, crumbling
> relics, and thrift-store paperbacks.

— 2   Use a colon after an independent clause to introduce an appositive:[41]

> They drank solar moonshine: a concoction of waves and particles.

— 3   Use a colon after an independent clause to provide an amplification:

> "Behold!" she said: feathers covered the walkway.

---

41   An appositive is a clause that illuminates or expands the clause just before it.

— 4 Use a colon after an independent clause to provide an illustrative quotation.

> We heard his ghostly words echo through the night: "Arugula! Arugula!"

— 5 Finally, use a colon to stick two very short sentences together if they are related:

> He was a grammatical neophyte: He didn't know that he should capitalize
> after a colon in America.

Last in the list of crucial punctuation marks: my favorite mark—the dash. (An *em* dash, not an *en* dash, or a hyphen.)[42] Use a dash to signify a sudden break, an interruption, a long appositive, or a summary.

> She liked the dash—but wait—did she really?
> She liked the dash—it was her favorite punctuation mark.
> She liked its frolic, its air of dishabille, its nonchalance—in short,
> she liked the dash.

You'll notice that the dash replicates much of the work of a colon or semicolon. It's more informal than either a colon or semicolon, but if you overuse it your writing can go downhill fast: Soon your work looks like one big interruption. Avoid the dash when writing scholarly work; it's too informal.

Remember: Within grammar's sacred bounds, punctuation is often a matter of personal preference. You might develop a love for semicolons. Or you might begin to rely heavily on commas or dashes—it just depends on how you speak naturally and how much of your natural cadence you want to portray in your writing.

An added note about exclamation marks: Avoid them. When I was very young I once sent a famous designer an excited thank you note, which he returned to me with all the exclamation marks encircled in red. A cruel response, but effective.

The Art of the Pause: Paragraphing

Paragraphing is a basic skill: The important thing to remember is to do it. Don't overwhelm your reader with page upon un-paragraphed page. Even the most focused reader cannot read on and on *ad infinitum*, always having to keep all the topics of discussion in mind, never stopping for a mental breath, never given a

---

42 In type design, an em dash is a measurement that matches the type size. So, the length of an em-dash in any 12pt typeface should be 12 points. An en-dash should be precisely half an em-dash, and a hyphen is usually slightly smaller than the en. Thank you to Robert Baxter for having memorized Robert Bringhurst's *The Elements of Typographic Style* (Vancouver, Hartley & Marks, 2012), from which this information comes.

pause to absorb new information. If you don't let them pause, your readers' eyes will start to glaze over, they'll miss the gist of your argument, the beauty of your prose. We're all distracted. I'm often reading student work in quite in a rush and find that I have an overwhelming urge to stop after eight lines or so if the writer has not paragraphed. I generally give in to this urge. Which is to say, I stop reading. This does not result in a great outcome for the student.

Begin a new paragraph when the idea you began has ended or reached a natural pause. Read your writing out loud—you'll notice that you stop for a breather at certain places whether there's paragraphing marked or not. Paragraph at those places. As you become aware of your paragraphing, you'll find you want to start new paragraphs as you move through your idea. Do not repress this desire. End your paragraph with a sentence that hooks it to the next one, closely relating the two. This "hooking on" sentence is called a "transitional sentence" or a "transition." More paragraphing is better than less, especially in academic writing, which requires so much of the reader.

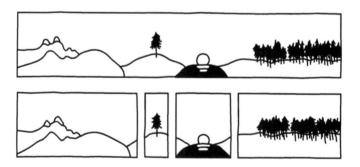

fig 5.2

Finding the natural breaks in a narrative.

When graduate students are first grappling with the very large amount of reading that they are called upon to do, I often suggest that they read just the first sentence of each paragraph of the book or article, get through the whole piece and understand its shape, then go back to those sentences that seemed valuable, and read those paragraphs. This is an effective way to get through a lot of reading. Keep it in mind when you're writing. Make it easy for your readers to scan your text quickly. Tell them what you're going to talk about in that first sentence of the paragraph. This will also help you edit your writing. Just order your paragraphs according to the flow of the argument in the topic sentences.

When you're writing, you may find that your mind works backwards, starting with details and ending with overarching statements. Edit your paragraphs

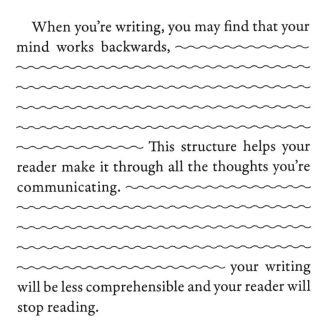

When you're writing, you may find that your mind works backwards, ~~~~~~~~~~~~~~ ~~~~~~~~~~~~~~~~~~~~~~~~~~~~~~~ ~~~~~~~~~~~~~~~~~~~~~~~~~~~~~~~ ~~~~~~~~~~~~~~~~~~~~~~~~~~~~~~~ ~~~~~~~~~~~~~~ This structure helps your reader make it through all the thoughts you're communicating. ~~~~~~~~~~~~~~~~~~~~~~ ~~~~~~~~~~~~~~~~~~~~~~~~~~~~~~~ ~~~~~~~~~~~~~~~~~~~~~~~~~~~~~~~ ~~~~~~~~~~~~~~~~~~~~~ your writing will be less comprehensible and your reader will stop reading.

fig 5.3

The first line of this paragraph sets up a simple observation. The middle section turns the observation upside down and tells us what to do instead. The paragraph ends with a clear conclusion: The defined mistake should be avoided.

after you've first drafted them. Put the general sentences on top, the specific sentences lower, the examples lower still. In this way, your reader will repeat the experience of going from general to specific over and over. This structure helps your reader make it through all the thoughts you're communicating. If you start one paragraph with details and another with a broad universal, unless you're really an experienced writer, your writing will be less comprehensible and your reader will stop reading.

Your topic sentences don't need to read like the first sentence in a Wikipedia entry, but they do need to contain a general assertion. The more imaginative your piece, the more you need to pay attention to the way your paragraph's structure echoes the sense of what you're writing. In his book *Ulysses*, it would have been ridiculous for James Joyce to order his sentences in regimented, outline form, since the book is all about enigma and allusion. But his work is highly constructed—you just don't see the structure until you really dig. The more expository your piece, the more the links in your chain of thinking must be apparent. The more fanciful, the more they can be hidden. But they must still be there.

This seems like a good time for a word of advice: When writing for instructors, make a big effort to reread your work at least three times to get paragraphing, obvious grammatical issues, and punctuation under control. Just read through once for each thing: once for paragraphing, once for grammar, once for punctuation. Do not turn in something you have not reread at least three times. Instructors are sensitive creatures, and they get offended by sloppy work. It makes them feel disrespected. They're also vindictive creatures, and may vent that frustration upon your head. Let's just say that I have Kleenex in my office, and it's not for my own use.

BRUSH UP ON YOUR USE OF ARTICLES

In English, an "article" is a word that clarifies how a noun is being used. (The most common articles are "a," "an," and "the.") For instance:

> I thought about *toenails.*

We haven't really narrowed it down. We're in the general land of toenails.

> I thought about *a toenail.*
>
> I thought about *an* attractive *toenail*

"A" is the *indefinite article.* ("An" is used when the next word starts with a vowel.)

See how this sentence is slightly more clear? With "a" we know we have only one toenail in mind. But we still aren't sure which one.

> I thought about *the toenails* of the two-toed sloth.

"The" is the *definite article*. Notice how the specificity of the sentence is getting more and more focused. "A" brings us in, "the" brings us even closer. If your first language is an Asian language or Russian, using articles can be one of the most challenging issues in writing English. Take it slowly. Learn one or two correct uses of articles, and then broaden out, using different nouns.

EXERCISE FOUR
Building Paragraphs

This exercise is 5-30-5 repeated in as many sessions as you need to complete it.

Begin your five-minute meditation, entering your mental writing space.

You have created seven beautiful sentences. Now you'll sketch a paragraph around each of these sentences. One of your sentences might be right for a topic sentence; one may work as an example, one might be good as a "transitional" sentence.

Sketch out seven paragraphs using this diagram as a guide.

Decide where the first of your beautiful sentences should go in the first paragraph. What idea needs to go above that first beautiful sentence? What ideas go below? If your original sentence fits at the end of a paragraph, what's an idea that leads to it?

Write/Sketch in the ideas: Each idea gets a piece of the diagram. Once you've sketched out the ideas you need to make a complete paragraph around each of your beautiful sentences, write those sentences. Try different arrangements until you feel the flow is good.

This first exercise in diagramming ideas has a bit of a pin-the-tail-on-the-donkey quality, so just approach it in that spirit and mash everything around until the ideas flow well. It's impossible to do this perfectly. Remember to make the new sentences beautiful. No extra words. No puffing up. You're spending most of your time on the diagram, sketching what needs to go where, doodling and jotting notes about what could go in those sentences, and then writing simple, clear prose. You'll have seven paragraphs at the end of this assignment. None of them must go together, but they might.[43]

Break this patterning and writing into thirty-minute sessions, with five minutes going in and coming out of your writing each time. Between sessions, get up, walk around, feed yourself, drink water, or stretch out on the floor. Then come back to the desk and start in on your next session.

This assignment will take longer than you're accustomed to sitting.

In future, you probably won't have the time to be patterning out every sentence of every paragraph you write. ("What a luxury that would be," she said, wishing she could be doing so, right now.) But do it here to get the music and rhythm of good sentences in good paragraphs into your unconscious.

We have done it. We have reviewed the grammatical rudiments many design students never get. If you learn these, you'll have most of what you need to be a good writer. For finer points and for horrible gaffs, see the appended *Grammar Tips and Eleven Errors of Death*, which appear at the end of this book.

---

43 My use of "none" here reminds me to remind you that "none" is a singular noun. It's actually a contraction of the words "no one," so mentally replace "none" with "no one" when you deploy it. You'll be saying things like, "None of these petunias is the shade of ochre that I imagined it would be."

CHAPTER SIX

Thinking in Diagrams

WE LIVE IN AN ODD TIME. With occasional breaks for a hike through the hills or a bike trip through lavender fields, we inhabit a world drenched in science and technology. Our experience of this world is one that no human in the 120,000-year history of humankind could have imagined, even in the last few hundred years, when scientific thought first started unfurling its tendrils.

The scientific belief system, a philosophy built on pushing for understanding through hypothesis, controlled methodology, and repeatable experiment, has altered our view of the world in enormous ways, ripping us from our pre-science notions of humankind's centrality in the universe. But this young scientific view has also provided new pathways for thinking about existence, ideas about individual achievement, new ways of identifying ourselves—of finding meaning in life. The scientific ordering of the world has pushed us to experiment and to note down our findings. It's asked us to hypothesize about what and who and where and how we are—and to persevere in questioning.

At the base of all this experimenting and documenting and asking and repeating lies the humble diagram. Diagrams are relatively simple sketches that tell us how an arch stays up or how the code will flow or how a molecule is put together. But they are also "not a representation of something, but the thing itself," as Reviel Netz once wrote.[44] They explain something to us without our having to have a physical experience. Diagrams describe process and change in visual terms. They are pictorial representations of how things work: how to put the patio umbrella together—where to find the WiFi network name on the back of the router, or how to build the paragraph.

Without diagram, no "Age of Technology" would have happened. You wouldn't be sitting there wondering whether to microwave a container of soup or to order take-out. Someone designed the diagrammatic flow-chart for the soup production line. Someone followed a diagram to put your microwave together. Someone created a wireframe for the food-ordering app. The human drive to describe process with diagram has molded our world—and the processes that mold our world mold us. Reading, viewing images, and decoding diagrams are three ways that our culture teaches us how to think about reality—how to encounter it, what to believe about it.

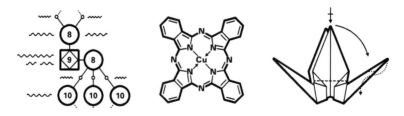

fig 6.1

Different kinds of diagrams.

In my experience, diagram is the method of transcribing most suited to design and design students. Diagrams describe change, and much of design is the imagining of change. Design is not production. Designers do not make each of a thousand chairs or each of a million tires. They gesticulate toward the future, waving a prototype of a chair or a tire—and they use diagrams to explain their imagined future to the producers of that future.

---

44 Reviel Netz quoted in *The Culture of Diagram*, John Bender and Michael Marrinan (Stanford: Stanford University Press, 2010).

Oddly, much of writing is also the imagining of change. Wallace Stegner claimed that the only requirement for a short story is that something changes between the beginning and the end of the written piece. No big plot is necessary, no huge idea must unfold; something is just different at the end of the piece from the way it was at the beginning. The same can be said of all other kinds of writing. All writing incorporates change—it is the description of a change. Poems, songs, project proposals—all alter the reader's consciousness between the beginning of the text and its end. You explain something never before explained. You ask the reader to think in a new way about something old. You put two things together that have never been put together before; you unearth a tidbit about some artifact that hadn't made it into history until you said it was important. All of this writing describes change, and it creates change in the reader.

So, you can see why diagram, which is a descriptor of change processes, is the designer's edge when it comes to writing. As we discussed earlier, you have a natural ability to translate ideas into pictures. You're used to making drawings, images, charts, graphs, and the occasional infographic, Lord help us.[45]

Using diagram is natural to designers, because it captures the process of visualization. It allows you to avoid the curse of enforced linearity and to sketch imagined connection and relationship in all directions. It's the tool for the mind that doesn't run on a linear track.

Basic mind mapping, that design school standby, is an exercise in a kind of diagram.[46] There's a reason your teachers "introduce" it to you over and over: Mind mapping is valuable for your design process because it allows you to capture all kinds of synapse-firings without having to put them in a linear or hierarchical order. This simple intuitive diagram allows you to step back and relate your mind's seemingly unrelated ideas and then gives you a chance to scratch out the obvious in your thinking—to hop over assumptions and "appropriate" answers quickly—as nimbly as a toad over a stone.

But back to writing. In this book, instead of using traditional writing outlines, we use diagrams to identify what is most important and what is least important, what goes out and what stays in, what goes where. You'll feel more like you're

45 I've seen enough infographics for a lifetime. Not real diagrams—those I love. No, infographics, which mostly tend toward putting facts in rounded-corner speech bubbles. Shall we all agree that this addiction to speech-bubbles must end?

46 If you're interested in pursuing deeper work in using mind mapping to guide writing, I suggest Anne West's book, *Mapping the Intelligence of Artistic Work*.

sketching than writing until the very last stages of the game. That's the way you're supposed to feel, so don't start getting itchy, wondering when the real writing will begin and if you're going to have time to do it. As you make the diagrams and jot notes in them, you're creating the architecture and assembling the thoughts you'll include in the final writing. Diagramming your way through the thinking gets you most of the way through the process.

fig 6.2

The mind map structure.

Talking about diagramming and process remind me of the time a designer friend told me that he was going to repaint his dining room. After waiting a few days, I went over to see his progress.

His house had seen many, many layers of paint in its hundred years, and I expected to have a nice cup of tea, then spend a few minutes oohing and ahhing over the great job he had done on the fresh coat of paint. But no. There was no paint. He met me at the door with a wild look in his eye and a wall grinder in his hand. He had spent the week skim coating the dining room, then buffing the new plaster to a creamy softness.

No new paint, but the dining room glowed like the inside of a seashell. Every inch of those walls felt soft, like sea-tumbled beach glass. As we chatted, he brushed his hand in a long, slow arc over one of the walls, enjoying the cool smoothness, feeling for evenness. He had made prepping the walls into its own separate, complete thing—made it as important as the painting would be. The final coat of paint took little time, and was a simple act, since the plaster underneath was perfect, seamless, smooth.

That's the way to approach writing with diagrams. Use your time mapping, finding underlying structures, filling in details, reordering ideas, plastering,

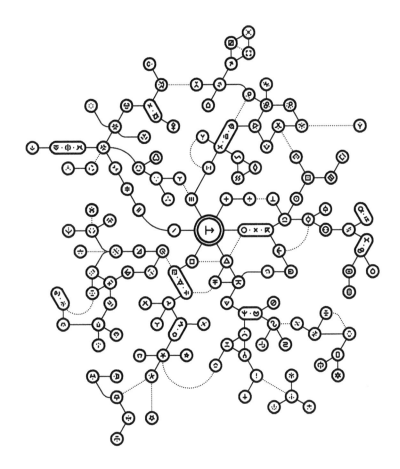

fig 6.3

A mind map is a transcription of your thinking. Open-ended, ordered, or full of arrows and false starts, it's never truly finished because it's a living diagram that changes as you work through your idea. Although you'll be using words in your mapping, Robert has abstracted the diagram, using symbols, so that we could show a complex map in a small space.

sanding the whole thing down until it's soft and luminous. Then, at the very end, apply a fresh coat of words.

IMITATE THE WAY YOUR BRAIN THINKS: NODAL MAPPING

Mind mapping is the journaling of the diagramming world. It's a way for you to get down everything that's shooting around your brain. For this reason, as I've mentioned before, design teachers love it, and many would have you mind mapping every moment of the day if they could. It's a great way to break open the carapace of thinking to find the fresh ideas within. If you've never mind mapped before, just sit down with a big blank piece of paper, give yourself a prompt, like "things to include in my dream studio." In the center of the paper, write down the prompt and circle it.

Moving out from this first circled prompt, put down the next ideas you think of when thinking of your dream studio, using one or two encircled words to symbolize each, attaching them to the original prompt circle and to other circles with little lines, according to relationship.

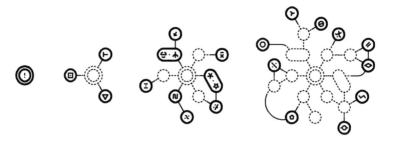

fig 6.4

Developing a nodal map outward from a starting point.

From this point, things will get messier, since each idea will prompt ideas, and the map will not be a regular sunburst. Keep adding ideas, and ideas that seem to attach to those ideas. Soon you will have a basic nodal mind map. Make sure not to put the brakes on your brain. Don't edit. No "too expensive" or "not realistic." If you suddenly write "Finnish sauna," keep it. If "blue tiled floor" comes up, keep it. If "long black walnut trestle table" comes up ... well, you know what to do.

Much as I enjoy a mind map, I find that in hands lesser than those of Anne West or my colleague Tiffany DeMott, the process can lose steam after the initial mapping. Instructors seem to think that after "getting it all out," the student will magically translate that stream-of-consciousness mapping into a cogent design or writing plan. This is where we must add in a step. Let's think for a moment about "rich clubs."

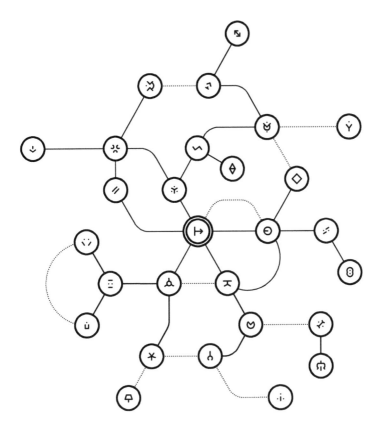

fig 6.5

*The Rich Club is made up of the essential ideas in your mind map. It is the mind map
distilled, and will form the basic structure of your argument. When writing, you'll
refer to your Rich Club (for the skeleton of your argument) and to the original mind
map behind it (for the details).*

In the last few years, Olaf Sporns, a computational neuroscientist at Indiana University in Bloomington, and collaborator Martijn van den Heuvel, a neuroscientist at the Brain Center Rudolf Magnus in the Netherlands, have been using graph theory to understand the brain's ability to synthesize what it takes in using higher-level thinking processes. They're most interested in a particular group of nodes, a sort of "superhighway network" of linked brain regions that may prove essential to our higher-order thinking. They call this grouping of hubs the "rich club network" because it's like a network of Ivy League alumni or world leaders at the G7 Summit—it's a network of nodes that hold the most power in the brain.[47] After finding out about rich clubs, I realized that the step missing after mind mapping an idea in the design process is spending time mapping the rich club within it. Where do you see the most powerful relationships? Using another color, attach those circles to each other. Do some circles seem to belong together? Attach them. When you look at the ideas in the map, circle the most important ones, the ones you come back to again and again.

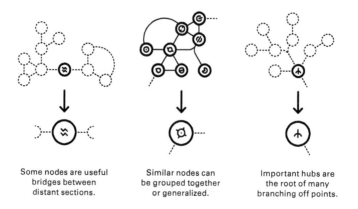

Some nodes are useful
bridges between
distant sections.

Similar nodes can
be grouped together
or generalized.

Important hubs are
the root of many
branching off points.

fig 6.6

*Patterns of
Rich Club
construction.*

Your mind map will start to create a secondary map of crucial information. By spending time relating your ideas to each other, you'll find your rich club—the most important ideas will start to arrange themselves, and you'll turn from journaling to designing and writing and begin to build the deep structure of your project.

47 Martijn van den Heuvel, Passim, https://www.quantamagazine.org/in-brains-rich-club-meetings-of-the-mind-20131024/ [Accessed September 12, 2017].

Trying Out Mapping

This exercise is 5-45-5.

Find a large piece of paper—at least 24" × 36"—a fresh black marker, and a fresh colored marker, preferably red.

Begin your five-minute meditation, entering your mental writing space.

On your paper, mind map your response to the prompt: "my dream studio."

Fill the paper with random but related ideas.

When you've emptied your brain of ideas and filled the paper up, stand up and walk around a bit.

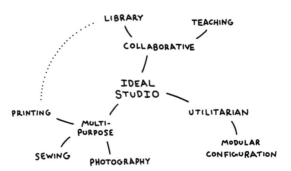

Return to the map. Now look for the rich club.

Where are the most important nodes in your map? Circle them in red, then attach them to each other according to their importance to you. Which ideas would you mention first if you were writing them down? Which second? Which third? Once again, we're experiencing that pin-the-tail-on-the-donkey quality. This is a messy business. You're looking for the most important nodes and the ways they work together.

Try different arrangements of nodes. How do the ideas relate to each other? Show which way the ideas flow by using directional arrows.

Make a fresh drawing of your rich club.

Exit your mapping work with your five-minute meditation.

CHAPTER SEVEN

Writing Is Argument

I BELIEVE THAT ALL WRITING IS A FORM OF ARGUMENT AND ALL WRITING seeks to convince. Learning to write is the process of learning to think things through—from the original spark of an idea, through the broadening of that idea, through the assembling of reasons or proof or examples of that idea, to completion of the idea. No matter whether haiku, email, article, epic poem, or essay, when you write, you're asking your reader to see things your way, to hear your story, to entertain your point of view—even if for just a brief moment.

Remember your first goal: Convince your readers that they want to keep reading—that they might discover something, find the skeleton key that unlocks the rusted lock. How many times, when I've questioned their dull introduction, have students said to me, "Yes, the intro's a little dry, but if you just keep reading it gets better!" How am I to ever see the "better" part if I have stopped reading during the dry introduction? Nothing happens if readers aren't persuaded to keep reading.

Writers argue to convince. It's not the kind of argument that means yelling at people or belittling them. The word "argument" comes from the Latin word *arguer*, "make clear or prove" and you're making clear and proving your ideas when you write. An argument sets forth a rationale with the intent to persuade–and all writers seek to persuade. Even a poem is an argument: It's a pithy little argument for seeing the world the way the poet sees it. Here's a translation of a haiku that Matsuo Bashō wrote:

An old silent pond ...
A frog jumps into the pond,
Splash! Silence again.

When I read this, I leave my reality and enter his. I see the scene that Bashō saw; I see the calm sheet of water, and then I see that fat frog slap into the pond. I see the ripples widen from the splash, and I see the calm slowly reassert itself. Bashō argues that life is stasis, change, stasis. I am with him seeing it—I am convinced.

The argument in a piece acts as an armature for that piece. It's not apparent, but it holds things up. There are infinite ways to argue—there are infinite ways to write. When you can discern the secret pattern of argument holding a written piece together, you're learning to read the way a writer reads. If you keep at it, you'll recognize more and more patterns of argument and begin to see them overlap and combine. When you practice deploying these forms of argument, you're learning to write the way a writer writes. When you diagram the "armature" of your writing, you're using your design mind to nail your argument down in concrete terms.

CLAIM   REASON   EVIDENCE   CONCLUSION

fig 7.1
Components of a linear assertion.

Most writers write using agreed-upon forms. Only experimental poets get away with abandoning form, and even then unconscious patterns appear in their writing. (English speech tends toward the iambic pentameter line.) But most writers mold their words and ideas into familiar forms, in order that the reader can get straight to the ideas, without having to cast around figuring out how to understand the piece.

Formal writing doesn't mean that you're sitting there drinking tea from your mother's wedding china with your pinky extended or that you have to use a similarly stilted way of expressing yourself. It just means that you're using an agreed-upon structure into which you're pouring your ideas. Humans have spent thousands of years concocting forms into which to pour their ideas. Forms exist for poems, for short stories, for expository writing.[48]

WHAT "EXPOSITORY" MEANS

"Expository" means that the writing you're doing exposes something—it discusses your idea, it describes your idea. In academia, writing is usually divided into "creative" writing and "expository" writing, which I find a bit of a false division because it assumes one is "factual" and the other is "made up." Good writing is good writing and it all exposes something. All your writing is "creative," whether you're synthesizing the driest of dry factual texts for your economics class or making up a bizarre adventure in an invented world. But, given that all good writing exposes something, essay writing is definitely its own art, and it's an art that, mastered, will leave your ideas behind on Earth when you're dead. Not to put too fine a point on it.

When getting used to writing expository pieces, the most important question to ask yourself is, "What do *I* want to have happen?"[49] Instead of being led by deadline pressure or what's available on Wikipedia, let *your* brain take the lead. What do I want to have happen? What do I want to say? And if you don't want to say anything but would rather eat cheese puffs and watch dumb TV, why is that? Make your boredom with the subject work for you. If you couldn't care less about a topic you need to write about, turn the spotlight on your own boredom and ask yourself why the subject is *not* important to you. Why isn't it valuable? There's something interesting hidden in your lack of interest: Write about that.

---

48 William Wordsworth once wrote a poem entitled, "Nuns Fret Not at Their Convent's Narrow Room," which is about the irony that strict parameters make creative work easier. He was talking about writing sonnets, but he could just as easily be describing a design brief. I'll include the poem here, because I want you to read it.

> Nuns fret not at their convent's narrow room;
> And hermits are contented with their cells;
> And students with their pensive citadels;
> Maids at the wheel, the weaver at his loom,
> Sit blithe and happy;
>   bees that soar for bloom,
> High as the highest Peak of Furness-fells,
> Will murmur by the hour in foxglove bells:
>
> In truth the prison, into which we doom
> Ourselves, no prison is: and hence for me,
> In sundry moods, 'twas pastime to be bound
> Within the Sonnet's scanty plot of ground;
> Pleased if some Souls
>   (for such there needs must be)
> Who have felt the weight of too much liberty,
> Should find brief solace there, as I have found.

The Poetical Works of William Wordsworth, Volume IV, ed. William Knight (1896), http://www.gutenberg .org/files/32459/32459-h/32459-h.htm#NUNS_FRET_NOT_AT_THEIR_CONVENTS

49 As in writing, so in life.

If You Missed Learning
How to Write a Five-Paragraph Essay

If my students have been lucky, somewhere between the sixth and twelfth grades someone taught them to write the basic expository essay. Unfortunately, research shows[50] that many of my students had their heads down and were doodling anime characters at the very moment that this crucial aspect of their education occurred. Because of this inadvertent tune-out, they never learned this most basic of essay writing structures and have gone along slapping papers together as though a pile of random words and quotes an essay doth make. Therefore, we shall start with learning this first formal structure, the beginning of the beginning in expository writing.

If you have never written a five-paragraph essay, or did so a while ago, do not assume that you're a smart person and so can pass it right by. Chop that wood and carry that water, for all builds from here. Force yourself to start at the beginning and you'll always know you didn't miss anything and will be able to take comfort in your solid writing foundation.

The Rooted Tree

Before we plunge into our five paragraphs, we must talk about trees. We're not talking about the growing kind of tree—we're talking about the mathematical kind, the kind examined in graph theory.[51]

Essays are systems, and the ways people write correspond to the ways that the brain prefers to interpret the world—to the ways that nature designs systems. The first—most typically human—way we organize our interpretations of the world into essays can be described as a very simple mathematical "tree." (The second way

---

50 I asked around in the Junior studio.

51 Brush off your math brain: In graph theory, a "tree" is an undirected graph in which any two vertices are connected by *exactly one* path. Any "acyclic connected graph" is a tree, and a "rooted tree" is a connected acyclic graph with a special node that is called the "root" of the tree. Every edge directly or indirectly originates from the root. The five-paragraph essay can be described as a simple "rooted tree."

**CYCLICAL GRAPH
(SEMILATTICE)**

**ACYCLICAL GRAPH
(TREE)**

**ROOTED
TREE**

we organize them is as a very simple "semilattice," which we'll get to later.) Using this concept, the five-paragraph essay can be described as a "rooted tree."

The essay starts with an idea, the root, which then branches to separate arguments, which are then traced to examples. Each point is separate and distinct and doesn't get jostled by any overlapping ideas. I'm describing the five-paragraph essay this way so that you can imagine its structure before I describe it in words, and so that you can understand a bit about why instructors love this kind of essay.

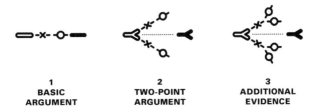

1
BASIC
ARGUMENT

2
TWO-POINT
ARGUMENT

3
ADDITIONAL
EVIDENCE

fig 7.2

Growing an argument tree.

The brain doesn't like ambiguity: The more confusing a city street, the less the brain will process that confusion. It will reduce what it takes in, and actually "see" less. Then it will make a construct of reality from those objects it has chosen to see. Similarly, if a problem is many-layered and complex, the brain cannot take all its complexity in at one time, so it makes "trees" of ordered thought. For the part of your brain that organizes complex thought, too much complexity reads as disorder, and too much disorder reads as disaster. The brain interprets disorder as a crisis—and it will do anything to reorganize information so that it can right itself.

Only in safe mental circumstances can the brain tolerate ideas that don't make immediate "tree" sense. Your reader's mind wants to organize your ideas into trees rather than to try to take in a confusing mass of ideas all at once.[52]

Writing about the organization of urban spaces, the architect and mathematician Christopher Alexander says:

> It is for this reason—because the mind's first function is to reduce the ambiguity and overlap in a confusing situation and because, to this end, it is endowed with a basic intolerance for ambiguity—that structures like the city, which do require overlapping sets within them, are nevertheless persistently conceived as trees.[53]

---

52 Which would explain why we're not all designing with overlapping type, *á la* the postmodern *Emigré* magazine of the 1990's.

53 From "A City is Not a Tree," by Christopher Alexander. Written by a mathematician and architect of urban spaces, Christopher Alexander's most well-known book, *A Pattern Language* has something of a cult following. If you believe that design can and should echo the complex systems of nature, Alexander is the design writer for you.

Writing in tree form makes life easier for your reader. If you have something very complex to explain and need your reader to understand every part of it quickly, and if you aren't writing something that could be more discursive and less direct, stick to the rooted tree approach.

The simplest essay form is the five-paragraph essay: State what you want to prove—a three-pronged argument—back it up in three paragraphs and finish it off. Mastering this essay form is an excellent way to gain practice in following an idea to its conclusion, something you rarely have time to do in your daily life. No one will pull out a phone and start texting just as you're getting to the crux of your idea, nothing will start beeping just as your argument is coming together. What relief. It's a luxury to be able to take the time to think an idea through in five paragraphs.

The five-paragraph essay is the starting place of expository writing. When you learn to write this kind of essay, you're learning to press your ideas into rationality. Rationality convinces rational people. It lets them open to your ideas because your logic leads them from one step to the next. Instead of just repeating your views loudly and insisting that you're right and everyone else is wrong—the sign of an untempered mind—you lead the way through your ideas, proving your points by using examples. If you're a thinking person constructing a rational argument, your reader will be a thinking person too. You're not going to attract people who just want to read a rant. And that's a good thing.

No matter how long or convoluted or complex your expository writing might become in the future, it will always do all the things this simple, five-paragraph essay does. It will tell us what you're going to discuss; it will give us your point of view on that subject; it will use examples to back up your ideas; and it will tell us your conclusions. When you get more comfortable with the forms of writing, you'll generally veer from the exacting requirements of this essay. But you can always go back to it, and, disguised, it can serve as the center of a more complex piece.

A FIVE-PARAGRAPH ESSAY, LINE BY LINE

The first of your paragraphs is called the "thesis" paragraph.[54] In it you "lay down" your idea. In the first sentence of your first paragraph, make a statement that

---

54 The word "thesis" comes from the Greek root τιθέναι (*tithenai*) "to lay down or place," via Latin, via Middle English. You're "placing" your idea in front of your reader.

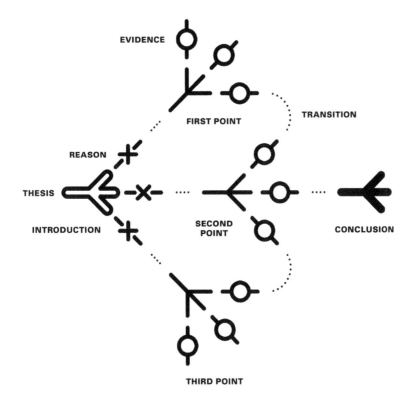

fig 7.3

The five-paragraph tree. An introductory paragraph leads to three paragraphs that develop the thesis and detail supporting evidence. These, in turn, lead to a conclusion, which sums up the argument. (Any similarity to bird tracks inadvertent.)

contains three points. For instance, I might write a sentence that states that birds are dour, thirsty, and annoyed in August. This is my thesis statement.

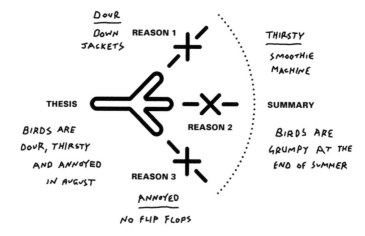

fig 7.4

Root, thesis, and introduction.

Continue the first paragraph with three statements that expand upon your thesis statement. Something like: "Birds are dour in summer because they're forced to wear down jackets. They're thirsty because it's difficult to find a smoothie machine small enough to operate with a wing. Finally, they're annoyed because they can't wear flip flops to protect their feet from hot asphalt."

Sum up the paragraph by restating your thesis sentence in succinct fashion, just to make sure people understand what you're about to prove: "For these reasons, birds are grumpy at the end of the summer." That's the end of your first paragraph. In a tree essay, the first paragraph is built the same way the essay is—it's a miniature version of the full essay tree. This cannot be said about the first paragraphs of other forms of essays.

fig 7.5

Self similarity in the tree essay.

The next three paragraphs go into greater detail about each of the points you've made in your thesis statement, backing up each point with at least three facts. If I were actually writing this piece about birds, this paragraph might first discuss facts about feather insulation and its inability to keep birds cool in extremely hot weather. It would continue by offering two other indisputable facts about heat and cooling related to birds. I'd end the paragraph with a sentence that hooks this insulation to the subject of the next paragraph. Something like:

"Not only do birds find themselves over-insulated in August, they also have a hard time finding drinks at this time of the year." This all-important "transitional sentence" makes your writing flow and allows your reader to follow your argument without jolting along as in a poorly-sprung carriage on a rutted road.

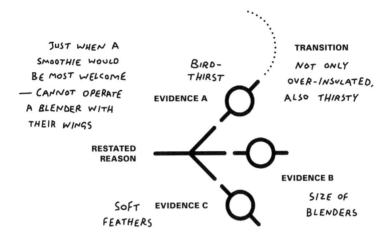

The next paragraph begins: "Just when a smoothie would be most welcome, birds find that they cannot operate a normal blender with a wing." Again: I would back up this topic sentence with three sentences about bird-thirst, the size of blenders, and the physiology of wings, all of which support my argument that birds get thirsty in August. End the paragraph with a sentence that hooks this paragraph to the next.

The fourth paragraph—same. State your third supposition, write three sentences that detail three facts to support it, and end with a final sentence that transitions to the next paragraph.

fig 7.6
A branch on the tree.

The last paragraph restates your thesis paragraph. After hooking the new paragraph on with a sentence that transitions out of the fourth's specifics and into your big idea, restate your first paragraph. Find a slightly new way to say it again. That's it.

fig 7.7
The conclusion and a return to the thesis

As we go into the essay writing, feel free to start using your computer. Many students find that they enjoy doing the exercises by hand, and they choose to stay with writing in their notebooks. You can certainly do that if you're comfortable with writing essays longhand. If you do go to the laptop, make sure to keep your notebook at hand. All the nodal mapping and diagramming going forward happens in the notebook, and it's a good place to keep scrawled notes to self. Or do your sketching on a tablet. Any combination of notebook, laptop, and sketching capability that works for you and that you can archive is good.

EXERCISE SIX

Master the Five-Paragraph Essay

This exercise is 5-45-5 × 3. In the first of your three writing sessions for the week, begin with your five-minute meditation, entering your mental writing space.

Set your timer for forty-five minutes.

Create a mind map response to this question: "Is Design Art?" Sketch a mind map of the words that appear in your mind. In another color, find your rich club. Using your rich club as guide, find an answer to the prompt and three reasons you are "laying" this statement "in front of" your reader. What are three facts that enrich each of those reasons? Jot these into the diagram. Fill in with notes to yourself about ideas and supporting facts. Don't write sentences yet. Below is an example of a filled-in diagram. It traces the development of Michael Bierut's essay, "Why Designers Can't Think."

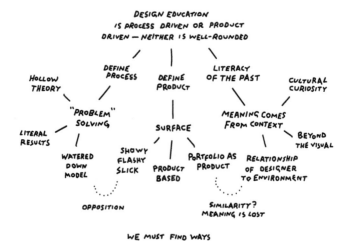

If you aren't finished in forty-five minutes, stop and pick up where you left off at your next writing session.

In the second of your weekly writing sessions, set your timer for forty-five minutes and either finish your diagram, or, once you've filled out the diagram, start writing sentences and paragraphs using the diagram as a guide. Don't edit yet.

In the third of your weekly writing sessions, assemble your first draft, rereading and shaping. When you have a complete first draft, start to edit. Make changes. Reread for grammar and punctuation. Make changes. Reread for paragraphing. Don't try to read for all of these things at once or they'll get jumbled in your head and on the page. Finally, use a spellchecker and then reread for words it has substituted in error. You'll be at a second draft. Time to turn it in and see what your instructor has to say. (I have students turn essays in twice—first as a draft, then, incorporating responses to my comments, as a final draft.) Or, if you're working through the book on your own, show it to a trusted advisor.[55]

You've written a five-paragraph essay. This is a big step in understanding the construction of essays and articles.

If you're going along diagramming and drafting and suddenly have a wild idea that you trust, write it down or voice-record it. This kind of sudden idea is good—it's a signal that your brain feels safe enough with the rooted tree essay structure to throw out something eccentric. Disparate pieces might unexpectedly fall into place, or you might want to scrap what you have and start afresh. Just follow your brain's lead. Give it time to get out what it wants to say. Note that down, then use the diagram to make your new thoughts into a cogent essay.

Lovely words can be strung into beautiful sentences. But those sentences need to work within elegant systems in order to support your ideas. The rooted tree of the "five-paragraph essay" is a good way to get your mind out of journaling mode and into expository writing. Keep this structure in your back pocket; it's useful any time you need to write a substantial few pages about one idea, and it can adapt to writing about many ideas.

---

55 If you are working through this book on your own, it is very important that you do not show your writing to anyone who has the slightest ability to knock the wind out of your sails. Hard as this will be, try not to show it to your romantic partner or a parent. Unless you are a rock-solid personality—and who among us is?—you'll be silently asking for far more than just a close reading, and you'll end up feeling resentful. Find a person who is bright, kind, trustworthy, understands your sensibility, and is not an intimate friend. Ask that person to read your work.

Most instructors expect that you'll use some variation of the five-paragraph essay when you write a paper. You might disguise it by putting a personal anecdote on top, you might lengthen it by stuffing it full of quotes and a few rambles and adding paragraphs with yet more ideas and examples related to the facts at hand, but the basic undergraduate academic form is that of the rooted tree essay.[56]

This tree is introduced
with two examples.

Some essays may have
sub-arguments in their branches.

Add things to a tree to plump it out.
This essay begins with an anecdote
and uses quotations as evidence.

Include your reader by opening
your conclusion to debate.
This tree ends with a question.

fig 7.8

An arboretum of different trees.

Try breaking up the structure a bit. Shake up the strict form by adding observations or secondary thoughts and ideas in extra paragraphs—always with the conclusion in mind and always pushing the argument forward. Let's not find ourselves wandering—just writing with a looser adherence to the rooted tree

---

56 We're talking about standard college writing instruction, here. Some instructors are quite inventive, and get you doing blog entries and tweet-storms and other things to keep you involved and writing. Tweet away, but make sure you learn basic essay forms to release your mind from the gnawing concern that it's missed a golden key somewhere and is not up to writing a more complex piece.

structure. In this way, your essay will become a more interesting journey for your academic reader.[57]

Think about rooted tree essays or short articles you've read that you liked. Map the author's argument. Did the writer start small, building up to a big, universal statement? Did the piece start by describing something universal, then come down to a small, but significant, point? Specific to general or general to specific?

The inverted tree leads with
evidence. The thesis statement
only appears once — as a conclusion.

Before you finish with this essay form, expand its scope by flipping the diagram, and instead of writing from general to specific, try writing from specific to general. Start out with seemingly unconnected "leaves," and follow them down to the root of your idea. This can make for a lively essay.

fig 7.9

A diagram of a flipped rooted tree

EXERCISE SEVEN
Flip the Rooted Tree

This exercise is 5-45-5 × one or two sessions.

Begin with your five-minute meditation, entering your mental writing space.

Set your timer for forty-five minutes.

---

57 Friends of mine, who have had a marriage that's been mostly as smooth as glass, once got into a terrible fight because of their opposite approaches to the creation of a walkway. They agreed that they needed to dig a bed for a stone path to be built from their driveway to the front door. She, a writer, expected him to create a meandering, curved walkway that she would then edge with lavender and rosemary in a Gertrude Jekyll sort of manner. He, an engineer and former naval officer, dug a ruler-straight path from the driveway, turned 45 degrees, and dug another ruler-straight path to the front door. Upon her discovery of this ruthless geometry, sides were taken. He believed his path to be efficient and therefore beautiful. She believed his path to be lacking in charm, discovery, or delight. Which path would you rather travel? Choose one and write your essays accordingly.

Pull out your five-paragraph essay diagram and your rich club diagram. Take a look at Figure 7.9, the diagram of a flipped rooted tree. Create an upside-down tree diagram with notes to yourself about ideas and supporting facts. Rewrite your tree essay ("Is Design Art?") starting with your specific examples and heading toward your general assertion.

If your timer sounds before you've gotten through the diagram, take a break and then set the timer for another forty-five minutes. Don't work for more than an hour and a half.

As you've done in the exercise before this, once you've filled out the diagram, start making sentences and paragraphs using the diagram as a guide. Don't edit yet. Then, when you've got a draft assembled, start rereading and shaping. Reread for grammar. Reread again for punctuation. Reread for paragraphing.

Spend five minutes coming out of your writing practice. Continue writing stints until you have a complete draft, then read it through one last time to find words that the spellchecker has substituted incorrectly.

So, we've seen that the five-paragraph essay and essays like it rely on a "rooted tree" structure—each part is related to the whole through a collection of subassemblies organized in groups. This kind of essay can be outlined, because it is a hierarchical and pyramidal structure. It's very much a non-fiction technique, and is especially suited to writing about design history or about your ideas concerning design. It can support a project as small as a five-paragraph essay or as large as *The History of the Decline and Fall of the Roman Empire*, a collection of enormous tomes from the late 1700s.[58]

I've spent a lot of time describing and walking you through the five-paragraph essay form. That's because it's a starting place, and because students I know have needed a full walk-through in order to feel comfortable with the form. We won't be going into such detail in later forms because you'll have a better understanding of the process.

---

58 Sir Edward Gibbon, who wrote *The History of the Decline and Fall of the Roman Empire* in the 1700s, took a rationalist and progressive view of history, so it makes sense that his book is a "rooted tree." He also made many asides to the reader in appended notes, which allowed him to speak in a more casual way, outside of the formal tree structure. He's considered the father of the footnote: For this we thank him.

At the beginning of this discussion of structure, I mentioned the semilattice approach I use to teach advanced essay writing. This way of describing essays is, I must admit, something I have stolen with both hands from the ideas Christopher Alexander describes in his article, "A City is Not a Tree," which is about the self-organizing systems of cities. Here, however, we're thinking about the design of essays, and how their systems work. This may seem at first as though we're going from the grand to the insignificant, but structure is structure, and systems are systems, and under a microscope a grain of sand looks mightily like a moon.

As we did with the rooted tree structure, we can adapt Alexander's semilattice idea to our current thinking about essay writing. Like the tree, the semilattice is an organizing system, but there the resemblance ends. The "semilattice" is an open structure, and its parts are connected to one another by many kinds of relationship, not just by one.

When we apply this open structure to essay writing, ideas don't have one and only one place they can go. They aren't immobile in their particular paragraphs, where we've placed them because of the hierarchy of the piece's argument. In a semilattice essay structure, smaller ideas can rub up against larger scale ideas and then again against tiny thoughts. Those "rubs" create secondary and tertiary ideas, without risking confusing the reader or disrupting the system.[59]

In his article, Alexander explains that a successful urban plan is not just an organizing of well-functioning mechanical systems that all work in isolation. He says cities' systems often combine in multiple ways, and that this combination is much more successful than a bunch of mechanical systems grouped together, each

---

59 Kandinsky divided the composition of painting into two kinds: the *melodic* and the *symphonic*. The melodic he calls a simple composition, "subjected more or less completely to a principle form." The symphonic he defines as a complex composition, "consisting of various forms, subjected more or less completely to a principal form," that is "hard to grasp outwardly." See his ideas abstracted below. We could describe the tree essay as melodic; the house essay as symphonic. (Wassily Kandinsky, *Concerning the Spiritual in Art*, [London: Constable and Co. Ltd., 1914])

MELODIC

SYMPHONIC

doing its one thing. Here he's energizing the idea of *gestalt*, which I'm sure your design instructors have thrown at you.[60] In Alexander's view, the whole of a city's systems is greater than the sum of its processes.

Adapting his ideas to writing, we can see that if you use a semilattice approach, you don't plan your writing by breaking your idea down into small parts that you then build into a tree. You put down your ideas as complete, independent units. These units relate to each other, and "support and enhance each other in a complex and interdependent whole."[61] This makes your piece interesting to read, because your reader's brain knows there is a system—and so is calm and open to ideas—but cannot immediately figure out the system, so remains engaged, making order from your "open ordering" of ideas. This technique results in a "discursive" essay.

This semilattice form is more complex to write than a tree argument is, but only because you have to have more of a hand in creating the piece's system. A tree's system is already planned out for you. With the semilattice, you're designing the system while writing the writing—a piece of writing that is at once attractive and clear—and you must be ruthless in your editing to make sure not have extra parts or tangents that do not relate to the greater whole.

So, you can see why this is a more advanced way to write. Do not engage in random discussions or digressions—no stepping out of your own plan, or the entire thing will come crashing down on your head. But when you succeed! You'll have a more interesting, richer, more complex fabric of thinking written out. And people are going to want to read it.

I leave the last introductory word to Christopher Alexander:

> In simplicity of structure the tree is comparable to the compulsive desire for
> neatness and order that insists the candlesticks on a mantelpiece be perfectly
> straight and perfectly symmetrical about the centre. The semilattice, by
> comparison, is the structure of a complex fabric; it is the structure of living things,
> of great paintings and symphonies. It must be emphasized, lest the orderly mind
> shrink in horror from anything that is not clearly articulated and categorized
> in tree form, that the idea of overlap, ambiguity, multiplicity of aspect and the
> semilattice are not less orderly than the rigid tree, but more so. They represent a
> thicker, tougher, more subtle and more complex view of structure.

---

60 The idea of *gestalt* is the idea that the whole is greater than the sum of its parts.

61 Quote from a complexitys.com blog entry, which I couldn't restate better than it was already stated, 16 May, 2013. Author: "Alessandro" at Abaco, Paris [Accessed 22 July, 2017].

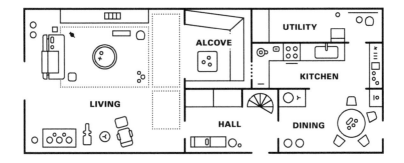

Deploying the Semilattice: Rooms Make the House

Imagine a house. Each room has its own function, but all rooms work together to create a living space that can accommodate many functions. The living room is a living room, but it also relates to the front hall, and it has functions that include welcoming people to the house. It also has a relationship with the dining room, and has functions that relate to the entertaining of friends and the doing of homework or the planning of projects. And although the function of a kitchen is different from the function of a dining room, what goes on in a kitchen affects what goes on in a dining room.

fig 7.10

The floorplan of a functional house.

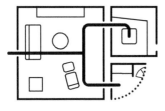

The living room is an open area — the adjacent alcove is more private.

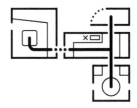

The kitchen can supply the dining room and alcove.

The entry hall provides access to both of the main social areas.

The utility room is hidden behind the kitchen, like a footnote.

The systems in a house are interrelated systems, and these systems are malleable. Design your semilattice essay like a house. Create small, yet interdependent arguments. The arguments all can combine in different ways; they can relate to

fig 7.11

Relationships of rooms in a house.

each other in the ways dining rooms relate to kitchens, but also in the ways dining rooms relate to entrance halls.

How do you go from mind mapping to selecting which rooms to put into your house essay? Look at your rich club. Use it to identify the core ideas you want to talk about, and the core relationships between them. Which of your ideas is a central room in the house? Which is a hallway, which connects more complex ideas? Perhaps you need a kitchen—a room that supports what's going on in the other rooms. Perhaps you'll be adding a pantry: an excerpt, anecdote, or statistical aside that supplies materials for other ideas in the piece. Examine each of your ideas and see where it fits in the house. Sketch them all out. Then plan the path you want your readers to take through them. Will they start at the front door? Or will they come in the French doors of the living room?

The reason that writing a house essay is more complex than writing a tree essay is that the writer doesn't start off by describing the house. You don't lay out what you're going to talk about and then knock points off one at a time, hierarchically, as in a tree argument. You create an argument, then explore it. You start in the dining room. You explore ways the dining room works. You explain the different functions it has in the house. You walk the reader to the kitchen; you explain how the dining room interacts with the kitchen. Then you walk back through the dining room and explain how it interacts with the entrance hall. You start in one place, then explore the different systems that you encounter as you move around the house. Readers begin to relate the functions of the rooms, and discover—and this is part of the pleasure of reading this kind of essay—that they're in a house. It's up to the reader to visualize what the house looks like in its entirety.

Danger lurks curbside. Since you don't start off trumpeting what you're going to do in a thesis paragraph, the reader is at risk. If the writer doesn't make good connections and doesn't describe relationships of functions and ideas, the reader will get stuck in the pantry or not be able to find the front door. You must give the reader confidence that your essay is a house tour and not a random walk with a crazy person.

How do you give readers confidence? Be clear about the structure as you navigate the house. Don't expect readers to intuit where they are. Tell them what you're doing. "And here we are in the living room, notice the light streaming through the windows." Let them know where the tour will begin and end. Tell them when you'll be stopping for snacks poolside.

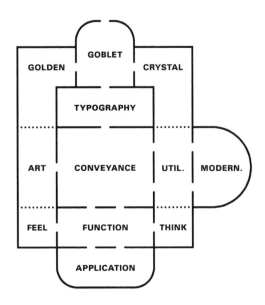

This argument begins with a simple metaphor foyer of a **GOBLET** to stand for **TYPOGRAPHY** and a pair of opposing concepts (**GOLD** & **CRYSTAL**) which will frame the main ideas throughout.

The thesis, **CONVEYANCE**, is a ballroom at the center of this house. It sits between another opposing pair: **ART** & **UTILITY**.

The third portion of this essay uses yet another opposition (**FEEL** & **THINK**) to discuss the **FUNCTION** of typography.

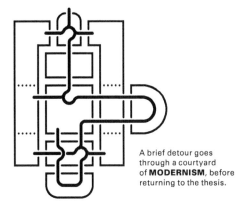

A brief detour goes through a courtyard of **MODERNISM**, before returning to the thesis.

Warde concludes with a review of how this argument applies to the **APPLICATION** of typography, followed by a return to the thesis

fig 7.12

The Crystal Goblet, *Beatrice Warde's discussion of typography, is written around a dichotomy, envisioned as the east and west wings of a "house" above. The main argument walks down the center of the house, peering into the wings from each room. These moments of "peering" balance the writing, allowing Warde to present two opposing points of view in the examples along the way.*

Of all the mistakes beginning writers make, being too subtle about what they're planning to do is the most frequent. There's something in a beginning writer that feels it's cheating to let the reader in on the plan for the words ahead. Somehow it feels more sophisticated to hold back and let the reader figure the structure out. But it's not. Do not hide in a closet, letting your reader wander around the house wondering what your essay is about. While you're waiting to jump out and yell "Tah-dah! Here's the big idea!" they'll have long ago put down your essay and picked up the remote. Be benevolent: Tell your readers your plan for the essay. This will not make them less interested. It will make them feel more kinship to you, and open them to your ideas.

Aside from being clear about the house tour plan, you might also work on your charm. Charm is underrated in our post-postmodern era.[62] Keep those readers in that house by delighting them, by creating relationship with them. Stuff those rooms with interesting furniture. Show how the turkey roasted in the kitchen will grace the dining room table. Make sure there are no slippery rugs between rooms. That way, if one of the rooms, or arguments, doesn't seem appealing to readers, they'll know there's another room right across the hall that might be more to their liking, and they'll keep reading.

EXERCISE EIGHT
Eight Paragraphs of House

This exercise is 5-45-5 × 3 sessions.

Begin with your five-minute meditation, entering your mental writing space.

Set your timer for forty-five minutes.

Create a new mind map and rich club on this topic: "Is Art Design?" Create a house diagram with notes to yourself about ideas and supporting facts for each room. The following illustration is a house diagram that sketches Kenneth FitzGerald's argument in his article, "I Come to Bury Graphic Design, Not to Praise It," in *Emigre* magazine, number 66.

---

62 Thinking of "charm" as manipulative is a hangover from the baby-boomer belief that "honesty" trumped all, which led to a humorless self-centeredness unparalleled in this century, and to seventy-year-old men in bike tights holding up the loading of the commute ferry in order to explain their personal needs for "space" to harried ferry workers trying to keep to a schedule. Recognize the plight of the ferry worker: Be charming.

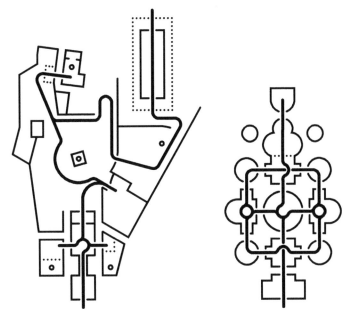

A piece of writing may begin in a very orderly fashion before exploring related concepts.

This heavily structured argument approaches a central idea from many different directions before continuing to an elaborate conclusion.

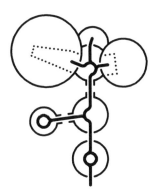

A series of independent ideas can be interwoven in a structured sequence to build a compelling, composite narrative.

A concentric house may spiral around a topic, exploring it one layer at a time towards an internal discovery or conclusion.

fig 7.13

Just as the methods of building houses are infinite, so are there an infinite number of ways to structure a complex argument.

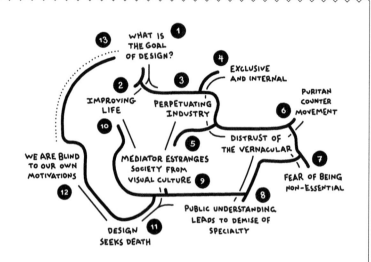

If your timer sounds before you've gotten through the diagram, take a break and then set the timer for another forty-five minutes. Don't work for more than an hour and a half.

As you've practiced before, once you've filled out the diagram, start making sentences and paragraphs using the diagram as a guide. Don't edit yet. Then, when you've got a draft assembled, start rereading and shaping. Reread for grammar. Reread again for punctuation. Reread for paragraphing. Don't try to read for all of these things at once or they'll get jumbled. Reread for only one at a time.

Spend five minutes coming out of your writing practice. Continue writing stints until you have a complete draft, then read it through one last time to find words that the spellchecker has substituted incorrectly.

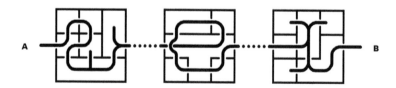

A TINY HOUSE CARAVAN

fig 7.14

A diagram of a "Caravan" argument

When you get comfortable with the hierarchical (tree) and discursive (house) approaches to essay writing, try combining them. Combining them is like creating a caravan—a train of tiny houses on wheels going from point *a* to point *b*. Each

80

tiny house is a separate home, with its own family and interrelated systems, but all the houses traverse the miles together in a linear structure, on their way to a destination. The "Tiny House Caravan" essay is a longer essay—you need the length in order to have the space to develop a number of little house essays and to arrange them all in a linear narrative.

EXERCISE NINE

Structure the Caravan Essay

This exercise is 5-45-5.

Map ideas on this topic: "The five artists and designers I've found most inspiring, are …"

Sketch a tiny house essay for each designer or artist you plan to include each argument. Diagram them. Plan examples for each little essay. Figure out how to arrange the tiny house essays so that they make a story, and your caravan has a beginning, a middle, and an end. Make sure all your house arguments are related and that each tiny house has the same destination in mind. The destination is your conclusion.

EXERCISE TEN

Write the Caravan Essay

This exercise is 5-45-5 × as many sessions as needed.

You've done all the structuring. Now write the piece. Structure your writing times in forty-five minute increments. Take it one house at a time. Take breaks. This piece has five tiny houses in it, and each tiny house might be five hundred words long. When you add an introduction and a conclusion, the piece will be about 3,000 words.

Once you've tried these three methods of constructing an essay, you'll have a nice bouquet of ways to approach expository writing. Soon you'll have favorite ways of creating patterns of argument, and those will become part of what people call your "voice," in just the way that your favorite ways of solving design problems become the hallmark of your designing. When you keep at it, choosing which technique you use for what kind of essay becomes second nature: You begin to know when to use what method without thinking about it consciously. Your essay writing—though never easy if you're serious about it—will become a solid, comfortable skill.

A Note on Conclusions

No matter what system you choose to present your ideas, examples, and arguments, remember to plan a chunk of time for writing your conclusion. Although teachers of the five-paragraph essay tell you to "restate your thesis statement" in your conclusion, many students interpret that direction incorrectly and literally restate their thesis, rather than rephrasing it. They say the exact words again, rather than dreaming up a new way of saying them. Personally, I think this is just a confusion, because who in their right mind would truly believe that anyone wants to read the same paragraph twice? Make a clean finish: "Stick the landing," as my colleague Silas Munro says.

Restate, but add in what you've learned during writing that tree essay that you didn't really know at the beginning. Or, if you're involved in a house or a caravan, leave your readers with a summation of what you think should be remembered from the ramble they just went on with you. Ask a question. Something that will stick in their minds. Don't assume that a conclusion must be dry and lifeless. Like a sprinter who hits that finish line tape at the fastest possible speed, save some energy for those last few seconds.

Right now, I happen to be listening to Mozart's "Piano Trio No. 2 in G Major." He's restating a theme as I write. This last movement is full of restating: It's a big basket of repetition. Mozart's playing around, adding in fillips and pauses and changes in tempo right here at the very end—just to keep us listening. I know you're rushed and your essay's conclusion seems like the final hurdle before you turn in the piece. It's the last thing you want to take slowly. But think about Mozart. He was late on his deadline for writing *The Marriage of Figaro* when he wrote this piano trio for some extra cash on the side. He had debts and other things due, just like you do. But you'd never know it from that trio's last movement. It's light. It's joyful—it's charming—when his circumstances were anything but. Be Mozart: Make us feel that of all the places you might be, this is the place that you most want to be, ending your essay with us.

CHAPTER EIGHT

Convincing

A S MY OLDER SISTER GRADUATED from the Department of Rhetoric at U.C. Berkeley, I sat, a bored teenager, fanning myself with the program and listening to the commencement speaker. Most commencement speakers are instantly forgettable, and I have heard many, many commencement speeches since then and forgotten them all, but this speaker, an intense young professor clearly chosen for his verve, said something that day that I never forgot. Standing at the podium, defining the arcane field of rhetoric for the graduates' relatives, he made a comparison. "Lovemaking is rhetoric," he said, "Rape is not."

Never was a field defined so succinctly.

When he made this statement, I stopped fanning, sat up and took notice. It was partially my age—anything about lovemaking seemed particularly interesting in those days—and partially the breaking of a taboo: People didn't talk about rape in everyday conversation back then. The difference between lovemaking and rape? By that age I knew well that they weren't related. Rape was not about sex, not about communication, but merely brutality, a physical power play. But lovemaking—that sweet, long-ago word—what about it could be considered rhetorical? I had thought that my sister's degree was about learning to write speeches. I remember thinking there might be more to this "rhetoric" thing than I had thought, and that I should look into it.

Rhetoric is "the art of persuasion," and it was honed into an educational methodology by the Sophists, around 2600 years ago. In Greece, most "convincing" of the populous was done in speeches. These days, most is done online, on paper, in films or on TV.

Aristotle first explained the ways people can be persuaded and taught people how to do it. (We ourselves are about to turn to him for the basics.) His student Plato, on the other hand, felt the teaching of persuasive techniques to be manipulative and, when mastered by the wrong people, immoral. This disagreement between Aristotle and Plato has carried forward for hundreds of years: People since have taught these techniques, and, at the same time, felt that there was something not quite right about teaching them. Convincing people that another group is their enemy, that that enemy is soulless, convincing them to fight, or—in lesser but still powerful ways—convincing them that they really don't want health care or that another group's ideas are threatening their way of life—all these political strategies are accomplished through rhetoric. Conversely, convincing people to get themselves checked for skin cancer, diabetes, or high blood pressure; getting them to join a march against injustice; or explaining the benefits of bicycling to work are also all accomplished through the use of persuasion—of rhetoric.

Often, the words in political speeches and advertising become dull, lifeless, and clichéd. That's why the word "rhetoric" is often used to mean the platitudes and routine saber-rattling of political speech. But there's more to rhetoric than CNN's latest panel of political experts, speaking routine words about long-argued issues.

According to Kenneth Burke, a literary critic and rhetorician, people engage in rhetorical process every time they produce meaning.[63] Burke says that our reality is built up for us by symbols, that it's:

> ... a clutter of symbols about the past combined with whatever things we
> know mainly through maps, magazines, newspapers, and the like about the
> present.... Calling for help is an act of rhetoric. Rhetoric is symbolic action
> that calls people to physical action.[64]

If this is true, then we can certainly make a case for lovemaking being a rhetorical state. From first presented rose to morning-after pancakes, the rituals of romance are symbolic actions that call people to physical actions.

As a designer and writer, you transfer meaning from one place to another. You call people to action, whether that action is buying soap or saving the wetlands. There is no design without persuasion, whether in minor ways—like being able to pitch a client convincingly—or in major ways, like designing a slim, oblong, rounded-edged, hand-held computer, the features and feel of which are

---

63 Burke thought about many of the subjects addressed in the constructed explanatory system of my beloved semiotics but found voice for these ideas in the constructed explanatory system of rhetoric, an entirely different intellectual "language." Being able to look at a problem through the lenses of different explanatory systems in order to test your own ideas is one of the benefits of education.

64 All the short quotes and ideas in this paragraph are quoted *passim* from Kenneth Burke, "Definition of Man," in *Language as Symbolic Action* (1966). Avoid dismissing the thinking of people who lived before you. The only difference between us and them is that their phones had fewer features.

so seductive that we all now have one glued to our hand at all times. You didn't just decide one day to buy your iPhone: You were persuaded to do it. No one used brute strength to overpower you. You were not bludgeoned and forced. You were convinced by rhetorical techniques applied to the creation and marketing of physical objects that act as symbols in our culture.

Writing is a combination of logical argument and persuasive device. At the very least, good writing persuades you to keep reading. At its best, it gives you the opportunity to see the world differently for a bit, to ponder both sides of an argument, to examine all the aspects of a problem. Good persuasive writing—ethically good—gives you a choice, and allows you to make up your own mind. But bad—ethically bad—writing also ends in changing your mind. It bludgeons you with repeated axioms and half-truths until you believe that they're true. That's the writing equivalent of physical brutality: it's battery, not persuasion. It's a strategy employed to use the reader like an object for the speaker's own need. When you give the individual no options, when you only allow one point of view to have merit, disparaging all others, you aren't writing: You're bullying. Don't do it.[65]

Rhetoric influences your readers' thoughts, changes their minds, changes the ways they see things, changes the ways they encounter the world. It's one of the cornerstones of your power as a designer and writer. We will now review the three most important ways that your writing must work if it is going to convince without stooping to threats and bludgeoning.

No matter what your essay's technique of argument—tree, house, or caravan—you'll always use at least one of the following modes of persuasion. You might use all of them. Aristotle coined the terms *ethos*, *pathos*, and *logos*, so this is not breaking news. But I'm often surprised at how few designers recognize these modes, and if they've heard of them, have not thought about how they always apply to their own work. Here's a review of Aristotle's three ways to persuade someone. We'll take them apart after first hearing from him:

> Of the modes of persuasion furnished by the spoken word there are three kinds. The first kind depends on the personal character of the speaker; the second on putting the audience into a certain frame of mind; the third on the proof, or apparent proof, provided by the words of the speech itself.[66]

---

65 Right and wrong, always a lively topic, is a binary I value, and, in this age of slippery slopes, a concept worth examining.

66 In *Rhetoric*, Volume IX, *The Works of Aristotle*, W. Rhys Roberts, translator; W. D. Ross, Editor, Oxford University Press, London, 1910–1931.

Ethos: Convincing by Inspiring Trust

You can pile up all the paragraphs you like and make them into trees or semilattices, but if your reader doesn't trust you, your well-thought-out argument is not going to be convincing. Much of this trust is built up outside the essay itself. The persuasive power of *ethos* rests on your reputation.

Your readers might trust you because other people say you're a legitimate authority, because famous people are quoted on the back of your book, or because a person they already trust trusts you. Perhaps they've had experiences like yours, or they've survived things you've survived and recognize their experience in yours. All of these are aspects of *ethos*, an attempt by you to win your reader over through a display of your good character. This is not as crass as it sounds. Look at any writer or designer you admire: How much of what you appreciate in that person's design is driven by your admiration of that person's character?

When you're designing, you'll find examples of *ethos* in brand values and mission statements. In developing or maintaining a brand, the character of the brand is of crucial importance. Tide, the laundry soap, must only be seen in Tide-like situations. It must act like "our" Tide acts, be a good as our mother's Tide, and the characters seen holding it must be radiantly warm, kind, and Tide-like. Its brand strategists constantly appeal to our knowledge of this soap's stellar character.

How does the brand act in the world? Can Tide be seen to be supporting causes not Tide-ish? Do we see images of neo-Nazis using Tide? Can Tide be found in compromising situations, swinging a fishnet-clad leg, surrounded by low lifes and hooligans? No. Tide must maintain its spotless character, convincing you of its value, using *ethos* as its mode of persuasion. If you plan to use *ethos* as a convincing technique, you must have proved to your readers that they can trust you.

Pathos: Convincing by Appealing to Emotion

I find that the best way to persuade my reader is to be as much myself as possible, relying on my human responses and ideas to reflect theirs. This is a form of *pathos*, relying on emotion to make an argument stick. Humor, sadness, love, anger, fear, hatred—all of these human experiences find resonance in the reader. But using *pathos* as a mode of persuasion can go awry very quickly. If you're altering facts to spice up your "personal truth," if you're reducing people to enemies and

fig 8.1

The Lion and the Mosquitoes *is a fable about a lion who believes that, because he is so much larger than the average mosquito, a group of them will give up the water in their well. He assumes that his kingly character will convince them. Sadly, the mosquitoes are not convinced by the lion's efforts at persuading through ethos. They overpower him with their greater numbers, and he falls down the well lamenting his pride.*

non-persons, or playing the violin of the victimized a bit too long, sooner or later your reader will get the creepy feeling of being manipulated, and stop reading.

My friend Therese Caouette has worked with refugees, migrants, and displaced persons in Southeast Asia for more than thirty years. In this time, she's seen a lot of humanitarian aid fundraising design and writing. Much design for non-governmental organizations (NGOs) operating in humanitarian aid is smart, unbiased, and absorbing. But some she calls, "Flies in the Eyes," and neither of us can stand this kind of fundraising communication.

"Flies in the Eyes" websites and brochures depict pictures of ragged refugees (or starving children with flies in their eyes, or both) and the ad copy tells readers how miserable these people are and how to "save the day" by sending in checks now. This kind of advertising (used, unfortunately, by legitimate NGOs as well as illegitimate) is often racist and always demeaning to the people it purports to champion. It's a blatant attempt at *pathos*, meant to grab your heart and wallet.

It's true that in order for your writing to persuade readers emotionally, you must make them feel something. But don't disrespect other people in order to do it. Don't make the people you're fundraising for seem "less than" or treat them like objects to be plopped in front of a camera at your marketing whim. Human respect and connection is the key here. To be able to live with yourself as a writer, stay with true emotion when you use the *pathos* technique of persuasion.

Logos: Convincing by Appealing to Logic

Designers love charts and graphs, partially because they're diagrams and partially because they're convincing to the kind of person who is convinced by logic—or by things that seem logical. Designers are often these kinds of people themselves. In our technological era, Aristotle's third category of persuasion, *logos*, "the proof, or apparent proof," works well on many people. Fact-based claims, ideas that seem black-and-white (with no room for gray areas), statistics—all of these use the logos approach. If you want to persuade fact-loving people to change their minds, try charts and graphs, facts and figures.

Of the three kinds of persuasion, fact-based arguments are most persuasive to people who are educated in the sciences and engineering and to those who believe in their own ability to think things through for themselves. Interestingly, this belief in self can lead people down the garden path of thinking that they are more discerning than they actually are and into believing "post-truth" falsity. Just because a statement looks like a fact does not mean that it is a fact.

fig 8.2

In The Leopard and the Ram, *a young, hunting leopard comes upon an unfamiliar creature: the strong and clever ram. The uncertain hunter is afraid of this new beast and runs off to consult with his friend, the jackal, who chides his companion for running from such an easy feast. When they both return to eat the sheep, the ram calls out and thanks the jackal for bringing the leopard back for his family to feast upon. The leopard flees in terror, dragging the jackal with him. The ram, in his guile, has used* pathos *to manipulate the leopard's fear of the unknown.*

Conversely, people who are persuaded by facts often assume that others will be persuaded by facts also, when—in fact—this is not the case. These are the people who shake their heads, annoyed that they cannot "make you understand" their ideas or logic. *Logos*—using logic as the main persuasive element—does not work if your reader is basically an emotive, intuitive, unscientific kind of person.

For example: Because scientists are schooled in and convinced by the *logos* technique, those who study climate change long assumed that people would be convinced of their arguments' validity because they were able to demonstrate that their studies were conducted reliably. These studies had resulted in overwhelming evidence that supported their conclusions. Being convinced by *logos* themselves, they assumed everyone would be convinced by facts.

This did not turn out to be the case. These scientists were up against politicians who knew that using *pathos* (in the shape of class derision and fear-mongering) and *ethos*, ("I believe what my Senator says!") would outweigh dry, complex, fact-based analysis for their constituents. Going forward, if scientists want to convince more people of the climate situation, they must mix *ethos* and *pathos* into their arguments in order to persuade more people to act.

To use these three techniques of persuasion most effectively, mix them up. Think about putting one in the major persuasive role with the other two playing minor parts. In this way, there will always be an argument in your writing that will convince your reader of something.

In our era, talking about "the art of persuasion" has an off-key ring to it, mixed up as it is with our experiences of advertising and political posturing and propaganda. (Propaganda is the use of persuasion techniques to convince large groups of people, moving them around according to the desires of an institution like a government or political party.) Advertising has been called propaganda because it works in the service of the capitalist system.

Do you feel bad about trying to be convincing? It's something to look at. Designers spend their working hours making objects and logos and websites and user experiences that are bent on convincing people to do things. We want to convince them to think that this object is the object to buy, that this option is the right option, that this feature is the best feature, that this product is the one for the job.

Graphic designers spend a large amount of their time in school learning the techniques of propaganda. Of course, we don't call it propaganda in the

fig 8.3

In The Scorpion and the Frog, *a scorpion must cross a river, and asks to ride upon the back of a frog. The frog doesn't trust the scorpion, and details his concern that the scorpion may sting and kill him. The scorpion explains that if he were to sting the frog, the frog would die, but then he himself would also drown. Therefore, he reasons, it makes no sense for him to sting the frog, and the crossing will be safe. The frog agrees. Halfway across the river the scorpion stings the frog. The dying frog asks how the scorpion could have doomed them both, and the scorpion replies: "I couldn't help myself: it's my nature." The* logos *argument, while compelling, is overpowered here by primitive response.*

studio—unless it's historical, unless it's about imitating the Russian posters of 1920 in a history class or studio project. But every graphic design critique hones the persuasive power of type and image. Design uses line, color, shape, texture, type, and image to convey an idea to someone in a way that will convince that person to do what the designer wants, whether it's to live in a certain way, buy a certain product, click a certain button, or vote for a certain candidate.

If you don't want to do this, if you feel that you didn't get into design to be manipulating people, you need to think seriously about it. Yes, designing can be flagrant manipulation. But you can find a path that is not just selling new widgets to people. You can use your communicative superpowers for good, supporting causes and beliefs that help living things. If you want to dive into corporate design, you can make sure to work for people you admire and for companies that have values similar to your own. Show "the conditions of the production" of your design or advertisement, reminding readers that they're viewing highly manipulated images.[67] Know what you're doing, and decide what kind of designer and writer you want to be. Uncover your true beliefs about your role in communication and make sure you can defend them to yourself. If you follow your own values, you might have to say no to a few projects, but you'll avoid regretting being in the business of convincing.

NO EXERCISE!

We're going to hold here for a moment and not have an exercise for this chapter. The next chapter will include practice with these persuasive modes. I imagine you could use a bit of a break from exercises for the moment.

Speaking of you—how are you holding up? Did you find a good chair? Have you been writing three days a week at your writing desk? Do you spend five minutes coming in and out of your writing? Have you found a good time to write? This might be a good time to regroup, make adjustments to your physical space and writing schedule—adjustments I asked you to avoid initially.

---

67 Jan Van Toorn teaches that a designer can always take a moral stance by "showing the conditions of the production." Show the edge of the white seamless paper in the photo shoot, to remind the teenage girl-reader that she's viewing a made-up world—that she's under the influence of a highly mediated image. I suspect Jan may have gotten this idea while under the influence of Louis Althusser, who once said, "Ideology represents the imaginary relationship of individuals to their real conditions of existence."

CHAPTER NINE

Tone & Voice

I MAGINE THE SCENE. Your professor, home from teaching, in thick sweater, wool socks, and large scuffs, sitting hunched in a large wing chair over a computer, surrounded by towering piles of unread papers. Perhaps a big bottle of aspirin sits on her side table. Perhaps she's nursing a hot cup of tea and wearing mitts and a parka because her island's electricity has gone off again. Perhaps takeout boxes are stacking up in the kitchen, because *there's no time for cooking—grades are due!*

No matter whether your instructor is teaching you design history or research techniques or how to write a design article, chances are that the poor creature (originally a person with nice shoes and a life, but now a harmless drudge) will read hundreds of papers in the course of your term. Hundreds of papers. Thousands of pages. She will be confronted by some very bad experiences during that reading. There will be bad syntax, there will be faulty parallelism, there will be run-on sentences. But the hardest experiences for her to bear—the ones that really grate on the old nerves—will be God-awful jumbles of tone.

TONE

When my ordinarily sweet and kind mother became annoyed at me for teenage backtalk, she'd straighten her spine, look down over her half-glasses and say, "To whom are you speaking?" in the frostiest voice imaginable. It put chills up the spine, let me tell you. This little Edwardianism of hers will help you remember what "tone" is. It's the way you choose to speak to your reader. To whom are you speaking? Choose a person or kind of person or group and write to that person and only to that person. Don't change your imagined reader in midstream.

You speak to different people in different ways. If we happened to meet in the hall, you wouldn't speak with me in the same way that you speak with your best friend in the studio. You wouldn't use slang that you knew I wouldn't understand, you wouldn't swear, you would use complete sentences, you'd listen politely while I went on an odd tangent, and you'd keep a smile on your face even though feeling lousy that day. Same with me. I would have my "professor face" on, and would do all the same things. That's because the *tone* of our conversation would be friendly, but slightly formal.[68]

When you write, you do the same thing: You switch tones depending on your audience. The tone of a love letter is different from the tone of an angry email to the electric company that has once again left you in the dark.[69] The tone of a paper or book or article depends on the relationship you have with your reader and on the purpose of your piece.

It's hard to explain to students why something in their tone "clanks."[70] Listen to your writing the way you listen to your music. Read your work out loud. Do you hear shifts in your diction, in your way of speaking, in the way you're explaining or conversing? Does it all sound as though you're talking to one particular person? Or do you suddenly switch audiences for a moment? If you do, you have a tone shift, and you need to correct it.

The Differences Between Formal and Informal Writing

When writing personal pieces, use a cleaned-up version of your everyday speech. Use a tone that approximates the way you'd talk with a colleague. This is called

---

68 If a student doesn't adopt a slightly formal tone with me, it's a signal that they may have issues with social perception. If you have issues with social perception—if you have Asperger's, for instance—work with your writing instructor to create a list of examples of different tones to use with different kinds of writing, then stick to the chart you work out together.

69 I'm realizing mine might have been the last generation to collect love letters and tie bows around them and store them under the bed. I suggest, should you not be doing this, that you start. When you are "old and gray and full of sleep," as Yeats once wrote, you'll be glad to reread those little packages of warmth.

70 "To clank" is a verb often used by editors. When something "clanks," it sounds funny and wrong in the sentence or section, rather than funny and interesting. It's an error of ear, really, like coming in sharp or flat in music. A word or phrase might clank because it's not the kind of word a person would say using that tone. It might clank because it's not your voice.

"informal" writing. Informal writing can include contractions, colloquialisms, personal pronouns, and sentence fragments—but everything depends on your ear. Did you decide to use the word "big" rather than "large" (a decision to be less formal) because of the way the word sounds in the piece? Listen for the music. Rhythm, texture, and opposition all have their part to play in good formal and informal sentences. Avoid jargon and slang because they will age your work prematurely as those words go out of fashion. Do not imitate accents—that can go very bad very quickly. If your piece is starting to fill up with big words, refresh the reader by using some down-to-earth phrases. Blend, blend, blend, as you would the shadow on your eyelids.

When writing letters to Congress, notes to your lawyer, or traditional academic papers, use a formal tone. Do not use contractions. Do not use imprecise speech. Do not use personal pronouns. Be declarative. Do not say, "I think that azure is a beautiful color." Say, "Azure is a beautiful color."[71] Formal writing is your chance to use words that your particular audience recognizes as part of its own culture. The word "interpretant" is not a word you would use in writing a note to your grandmother, unless she is a semiotician. But it's very comfortable in an academic piece for the Semiotic Society of America.

Formal and informal usage can blur once you become confident in the uses of each. The tone of this book is a combination of formal and informal writing. I'm using contractions, colloquialisms, and personal pronouns, but I'm also being declarative and using words I wouldn't use in everyday speech. That's because my reader is a designer or design student, a person who has attained a level of education that allows me to switch back and forth between design-speak, formal assertion, and informal discussion.

I prefer for my students to write as if they are writing directly to me, which is also a blending of formal and informal tones. If you're writing an article for a professional magazine or blog, take your tonal hints from the kinds of things you've seen in that publication. I would, for instance, write in the tone in which I talk with colleagues for a piece in *Communication Arts* magazine or *Eye* magazine, but I would adopt a cooler, more formal tone should I write something for the *Journal of Design History* or for the AIGA's *Dialectic* magazine.

Even when stressed and writing about something in which you have little interest, you must identify your reason for writing, remember your intended

---

71 My uncle Nicholas Boratynski was known for his aphorisms. A favorite, dealing with the importance of context: "Azure is a beautiful color, but not in sausage."

audience, and know what you want the reader to remember about your piece. These are all elements of your tone.

A Personal Tone

I write most of what I write in a personal tone by informed choice, not by predilection. When I began writing, I wrote in a traditional academic manner. I never used the first-person singular, never used a contraction or a colloquialism, and filled all my essays and articles with appropriate numbers of scholarly quotes. Everything I wrote was a mini-fortress, prepared for the attack of unknown assailants.

But one baking August afternoon I found myself in shorts and T-shirt driving an old Aerostar from Nevada City to Marin County. With all the windows open and the radio cranked loud for company, I picked up an NPR station somewhere around Roseville, tuning into the middle of an interview with Norman Mailer, the post-war American novelist. I had never been a Mailer fan, what with his stabbing his wife and all, but listening to the show, I enjoyed hearing his aging pugilistic intelligence and he said one thing that changed the way I wrote.

He said that when he was writing his first book, *The Naked and the Dead*, he spent hours and hours getting every phrase perfect, not out of his love of writing, but because he wanted to impress his critics. He wanted the critics to appreciate every brutal twist and turn of his language and phrasing. He thought they would be reading very carefully, looking at every word.

The book came out and there was a real critical brawl over it, and he was right in there, slugging away at critics as they slugged away at him. But he could tell that the critics hadn't really read his book carefully, that they were just piling onto the fight. So, after it all died down, after all the fame and after all the vitriol had been printed, when he had settled in and was writing his second book, he told the interviewer that he "just hoped somebody would read it."

Driving along on that hot afternoon, I thought about how I had been piling up quotes and building fortress-essays, not because I was enjoying the comparing of my ideas to those of other writers, but to be safe, to silence critics. It was on that road trip that I realized I needed to be focusing on my reader, not on my critics. I suggest you do the same.

I believe that, in the past, people had much more faith in the "objective truth" of the journalist and academic than they do now. People used to believe that this

Until more than two centuries after printing nobody discovered how to maintain a single tone or attitude throughout a prose composition.

ORIGINAL

McLuhan, Marshall. *The Gutenburg Galaxy: The Making of Typographic Man.* p. 154

After printing was invented, it took two hundred years for people to figure out how to stick to one way of speaking and to one point of view when they wrote something that was going to be published.

INFORMAL

Two centuries after Gutenberg invented the printing press, writers still had not confined themselves to maintaining a syntax or a cohesive point of view, which resulted in the absence of "tone" throughout their published compositions.

FORMAL

fig 9.1

Here, Marshall McLuhan states that the invention of printing changed the ways people think. He wrote for an intelligent reader of the 1960s. If he were writing for intelligent readers today, how would his tone be different? McLuhan was known for his quotable quotes. What makes his original quote more quotable than the informal and formal rewrites below it?

kind of writing was neutral and impartial, weighing facts and ideas with an even hand. But as children of the postmodern, readers today don't have as much faith in human objectivity, and seem to find more value in an honest, subjective account than in something that purports to be dispassionate and detached.

People open up to your ideas when you show that you're a person. Yes, it's a less defensible position than is striding around behind the third-person singular. But I find that students are better able to understand ideas and critical thoughts if they know they're coming from a person, and not from an anonymous, godlike voice. This strategy has worked for me. You will make your own decisions about the tone of your work, and I hope (as Mailer hoped for himself) that you win the supreme accolade, that someone takes the time to sit down and really read what you have written.

EXERCISE ELEVEN
Tone Warm-Up

From here on in I'm going to expect that you know to come in and out of your writing slowly and to work in short increments of forty-five minutes or less, taking breaks between them. For this exercise, map, diagram, find the rich club, and write a short 850-word piece—either tree or semi-lattice—about: "The reasons that design is the right life for me ..." Write in a personal tone, but make an argument. Pick *ethos*, *pathos* or *logos* as your primary technique for convincing. Pay attention to your use of sentence fragments and syntax.

A Professional Tone

What's a professional tone? Well, clearly, it's the tone you adopt when writing for colleagues. But, as with adopting a personal or formal tone, a professional tone requires you to use your "tone ears." When I write a piece for a design magazine or blog, I read a few pieces the publisher has already published and let the tone of that work sink in. Then I imagine that I'm writing to an esteemed, but not intimate, colleague (for some reason I often pick Lucille Tenazas, though I've never told her this) and write as if I'm writing to her.

As with the personal essay, the rules for professional writing are not set in stone. But it's better to err on the formal side than to get too cozy with your reader.

A softening of the formal tone, the use of contractions, yes. Slapping your reader on the back and calling him "Bro," not so much. No one likes a presumption of unearned familiarity. It's inauthentic.[72]

The wonderful thing about writing a professional piece is that you're writing to people who understand your designer language. This is when you can really let the design-talk rip. Most educated designers share a common parlance, having been schooled by Modernists and Postmodernists, and the opportunities to use this fairly obscure area of knowledge are rare. Their office mates are busy with projects, they themselves are busy—too busy to stand around the water cooler and engage in a discussion of *gestalt*.

So, now, when you're writing your design article, or design blog entry, or book—now's the time to stand around the invisible water cooler and use the words and language of critique, or aesthetics, or the most recent advances in design technology. But be careful about mixing them all together. And if you do switch from personal vignette to design concept to latest app, make sure to blend those transitions between paragraphs and subject so that the transitions aren't jarring. Blend.

Nobody likes a jump cut.

Professional pieces for magazines and blogs generally fall into three categories: the *personal essay*—often used by editors as a soft landing at the end of a magazine or in a separate section on blogs—usually about 850 words long; the *editorial*—a piece which relies on *ethos*, and presents a personal opinion but is written more formally—generally 850–1,500 words long; and the *feature*—a stand-alone story, generally written in a journalistic manner that does not usually allow the personal voice to intrude—which can be anywhere from 2,000 to 10,000 words long.

Editorials and features generally follow the journalistic rules of stating "who, what, where, when, and why" right up front. No throat-clearing allowed. Just start in with the facts, and fill in the details after you've gotten the basic situation down. Current editors tend to cut from the bottom of your piece, just as old-time newspaper editors did, so make sure the important stuff is right up front. This is a rooted tree moment if there ever was one.

Discursive essays—our house and caravan essays—tend to fit more comfortably in anthologies, academic journals, and books—places where the reader is sitting down with a glass of wine to have a slow and thoughtful mental conversation with

---

72 Sister Nicholas Maltman, O.P., once gave me some sobering writing advice.
    "Try to be authentic, not original."

you rather than frantically trying to get the facts and move on. Again, the tone here is one of conversing with equals. No puffery, no pomposity.

Writing for websites and emails is professional writing, but we cover them in their own sections later in this book, so go there if you're trying to write something for the web that's not an article, editorial, personal piece, or feature.

EXERCISE TWELVE

A Short Professional Piece

Make your nodal map, your rich club diagram, and write a 850-word professional article (tree or semi-lattice) about the most ridiculous belief current designers have about the future and why you believe it to be ridiculous. Pick *ethos* or *logos* as your primary technique for convincing. Use *pathos* somewhere in your article to deliver an emotional punch. Don't forget to footnote your sources.

THE TRADITIONAL ACADEMIC VOICE

Now here's a confusing thing: The traditional academic voice is actually a species of tone. This shows you how much these two ideas—voice and tone—overlap. Let's agree that when writing a traditional academic piece, you'll adopt a formal tone. To review, a *formal* tone is different from that of having a conversation or writing a personal essay, which is considered an *informal* mode of communication.

The formal tone of the well-conceived traditional academic voice avoids slang, contractions, and colloquialisms, and its language is crystal clear and unmuddied. It doesn't use big words just because they're big, unnecessary jargon, or academic clichés. It doesn't sound stilted or complex. In order to write in an academic voice, you must use third-person declarative statements, be authoritative rather than tentative, and avoid casual language and syntax. In truly formal academic writing, do not use "I" statements; use declarative statements. Instead of saying, "I think that Picasso was a charlatan," say, "Picasso was a charlatan." And then prove why, using *ethos* or *logos* as your persuasive technique.

In recent years, the "no 'I' statements" rule has relaxed somewhat, especially in the kind of formal writing that designers generate. If you're engaged in writing your PhD dissertation, I would counsel you to continue in the truly formal academic mode. But if you're writing for a Master's or Bachelor's degree, the "I" statement has a place in your writing.

Academic writing in design often rests on the designer's own experience, and to make "I" statements into third-person declarations of that experience can read as distant or pompous. Academic writing in design conforms to stringent standards for research, documentation, and exploration, but relaxes a bit in the writing of the narrative to include the value of the designer's personal experience.

VOICE

Tone is not the same thing as voice, although voice and tone often play together in the same sandbox. Your *tone* will change, you'll vary your diction and words when talking to different people—a group of designers, say, or a group of academics—but when writing becomes second nature your *voice* will not change.

Your voice is exactly that: *your* voice. It's the combination of beliefs and favorite themes and points of view and style and diction and grammar and particular ways of stating ideas that show up in your writing no matter what kind of writing you're doing. It's the combination of all these factors—the part that is essentially *you*. You know you've found your authentic voice when readers say, "I knew you wrote that piece—I could hear you saying it."

CHAPTER TEN

Academic Writing

I FIND THAT STUDENTS TAKE CALMLY TO WRITING PERSONAL AND professional essays. But when it's time to write something "academic," their fingers freeze to the keyboard. They tell me that the plain speaking I've been pounding into them just doesn't feel like enough. They feel they should be writing in a way that makes them sound smart to their instructors, using words like "intertextuality" and "praxis." They worry they'll be judged deficient if they don't write with words like this.

These students have a right to be anxious. Sometimes their design instructors want to be taken seriously—want to be appreciated for their ideas—yet don't write particularly well, so they load their own interminable paragraphs with words they've heard in grad school or have read in other people's articles in order to prove that their ideas are worthwhile, that they speak the language of intellectuality. Strangely, if you write in a simpler, more focused way than these instructors write, they'll appreciate your writing. They may never have had the opportunity to learn to write clear prose, and so will recognize the value of yours. In school, my design instructors often asked me to edit their articles and books, and after we threw out tons of big words and jargon, they always liked their writing better.[73]

But before you decide to write like Hemingway, remember: Not all good words are short. Not all concepts can be defined in words of one syllable. Design's

---

73 Try writing simply and effectively first. If worried about your grade, ask the instructor to read two paragraphs of your paper before you turn it in: Write those paragraphs simply, explaining something complex in a very accessible way. Get feedback. Adjust accordingly. Notice how the power suddenly shifted from the instructor's hands to yours. You can write any way someone needs you to write—you have the flexibility to do so. But when writing your own stuff—not meeting an instructor's expectations—keep to the clean, the elegant, the clear.

academic language can express difficult concepts with words made expressly for the discussion of those concepts. You think nothing of discussing "typographic hierarchy," because those words cannot be replaced by smaller words, so don't be afraid of the big words you might encounter in academia. Just avoid trying to sound smart, avoid overused expressions and clichés, and only use a large word when there is no small one that means the same thing.

At best, academic writing can explain the difficult and propose fresh ideas in clear, appealing language. At worst, it can devolve into a hyper-intellectual mix of phrases—phrases lifted from other disciplines—and lose readability, humor, kindness, conversationally, and simplicity. There's nothing more beautiful than well-written formal language and nothing worse than pompous prose.

As a designer, there's really no reason to write in a hyper-academic way. Design is not a hyper-academic subject. It has its feet on the ground because, at base, it's a profession and not an art. The best academic design writers do not write overly complex prose: Jessica Helfand's sentences are so clean they could give you a paper cut. Robert Bringhurst's poetic cadence will convince you to love type whether you want to love it or not. And Stefan Bucher tosses ideas around in ways that are at once intimate, fantastic and enlightening.

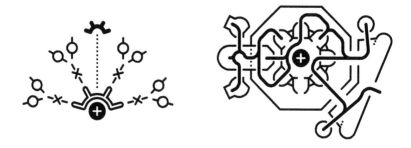

What Is an Academic Critique?

fig 10.1

Constructing the academic review.

To designers, "critique" means standing for hours taking a look at other people's work. That can confuse them when they're asked to write something called an "academic critique," which is a short paper or article that evaluates something critically. This is a tree or house argument written in a formal academic tone, which has at its center the work of another person. The five-paragraph essay is often taught as a first structure for writing a critique; the structure is so simple that you can spend your energy on your ideas about the person, place, or thing that you're criticizing.

Remember, criticizing is not being snarky. First, it's sleuthing out what objectives the designer, author, or artist set for the piece, then evaluating whether those objectives were met. Second, it's thinking about what the piece says about design as a culture and then what it says about the culture at large. As you become facile with writing critique, you may want to move from tree and house to caravan, stringing out small house arguments about specific artistic or design issues that come up in the work.

EXERCISE THIRTEEN

An Eight-Page Academic Critique

Create the mind map, rich club, research, and diagram for a 2,000-word academic article on a person or group you believe should be included in the history of design but who was not mentioned in your history classes. Why do you think that this subject was not included in the current curriculum? What is your critical view of the work of this person or group? Why should this person or group be studied by everyone who studies design? What does your research tell us about the work, how well known it is, about the ways design history education has been structured, or about why your topic might not have been chosen for inclusion in the "canon" of our design history? What does this lack of inclusion say about our culture at large? Write the piece. Footnote, footnote, footnote.

STRUCTURING THE COMPLEX THINK PIECE

Luckily for us, we've already discussed ways to structure argument and ways to persuade your reader that your ideas make sense. We've reviewed three ways to argue short pieces—the tree, the house, and the caravan—and three ways to persuade people—*logos*, *ethos* and *pathos*—and these can all be used as techniques for writing a longer, more complex think piece.

If you're writing about aspects of design that verge on the scientific—ideas having to do with big data, for instance, or with methods of production—you might start with a tree diagram and go to *logos* as your persuasive mode. If you're exploring a historical or contextual topic, you might begin with a house diagram and use *ethos* as your major persuasive mode. And if you're describing design research that centers on the experiences of others, you could begin with a caravan diagram, and use a combination of the *logos*, *ethos*, and *pathos* modes of convincing. To whom are you writing? Being very clear about your audience will tell you which mode to use.

Various and Oppositional Arguments

A "think" piece is an essay that centers around the development of your own ideas. Unlike a research paper or article, you aren't putting the focus on other people. You aren't comparing and contrasting other people's ideas and adding in an idea or two of your own. In a "think" piece, you're using other people's ideas to buttress or negate yours: But yours are the stars of the show. This is a quiet yet crucial distinction.

When you're engaged in longer, more complex writing, the pitfall of boring your reader gapes below you. With more words, you have the opportunity to examine an idea from more than one or two angles. But if you aren't careful, you can bog down into a sort of dull circling around and around of the same verbal track, varying the subject, but not the repetition of "idea, supporting matter, example." It is all about your ideas, and there's just so long that you're going to be able to spin your own thoughts without some oppositional energy added in from outside.

SYNTHESIS

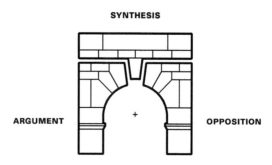

ARGUMENT   +   OPPOSITION

fig 10.2

An argument, its opposition, and a final synthesis.

That's why, if you're writing over 2,000 words, or eight pages,[74] though you may use tree, house or caravan as a first diagram for the piece, it's important to add in two things, opposition and synthesis, and to get them into your diagram as you sketch out your first ideas. If you're up on your Hegelian dialectics,

---

74 A page with 1-inch margins in 12-point type, double spaced, flush left, ragged right, is about 250 words long. A 2,000-word essay, then, is about eight pages long. Get in the habit of double-spacing line heights. Editors require it. It's far easier on their eyes, and it's easier to see their corrections and comments. So it's easier on your eyes, too.

you'll recognize a faint echo of the much-taught idea of thesis, antithesis, and synthesis here.[75]

In a complex think piece, you don't just tell people your idea and then show examples that support your idea. You state an idea, show examples of why this idea is valuable, then bring in an opposing idea, an idea that your proposed idea can smash a chair over to start a bar room brawl. Your original idea and the opposing idea duke it out, each showing examples and quoting people that say they're right—and finally, after they've smashed up the place and exhausted themselves, you have them to shake hands and admit that they can get along together after all—you have them find synthesis, or compromise.

Of course, the "compromise" is the idea you truly wanted to put forth in the first place. But all the breaking of chairs over heads is the action that keeps your reader reading and allows that reader to be in on the process, on the development of your thought. For, as you write, even though you've mapped and planned and sketched, your idea will change as you explore the thinking of other people. So, your final "compromise" will be different from what you originally thought it would be.

Bringing a first thesis, or idea, into contact with its opposite, its antithesis, exposes flaws in the first idea, and your reader will enjoy watching you arrive at your third idea, or "synthesis." For your reader, such a complex think piece is a rich experience of relationship with you rather than a dull plod in old sneakers around pages and pages of a darkling high school track.

EXERCISE FOURTEEN
Balancing Opposing Arguments

Create a mind-map, a rich club, and a diagram for a 2,000-word essay that includes a bar fight between your idea and an opposing argument.

What shall you write about? Why not examine your thoughts on this topic: "The most important thing design can do for people is ..."

---

75 Or, more exactly, on Heinrich Chalybäus's restatement of Hegel's dialectic, more often stated by Hegel as Abstract–Negative–Concrete. These days, many scholars feel that Hegel's idea about thesis and antithesis becoming a "whole," is not actually a triadic operation. We shall leave this conversation to the philosophers. For our purposes, Chalybäus's triad works just fine. (For more discussion of the triad in Hegel's dialectic: Gustav E. Mueller in Jon Stewart, ed. *The Hegel Myths and Legends.* (Chicago: Northwestern University Press, 1966).

Create a diagram of your rich club's (idea's) nodes. Arrange the nodes for your first argument for the piece. Sketch in plans for examples and quotes from experts for that first argument.

How would you argue against the idea you've just diagrammed? With another color, diagram an argument against your first argument, using the same nodes as your first argument but drawing its opposite. Fill in with examples and quotes from experts for that second argument.

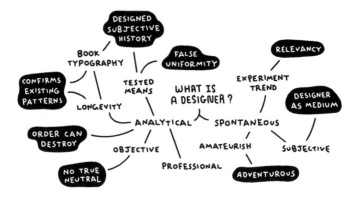

Now, time to brawl.

Set both ideas one node against the other, node by node, idea by idea, supporting with examples (*logos*) and quotes from recognized experts (*ethos*). End with a personal conclusion that contains a synthesis of both ideas and persuades using a light touch of *pathos*.

(When you write this, and you think it turned out well, send me a copy ℅ my publisher. I really enjoy reading what people write for this particular exercise. It brings so many techniques together.)

What *Academic* Research Is and Is Not

Research is not writing. It's a separate phase of thinking that happens between diagramming an idea and writing about it. Designers use two very different research methods: design research and academic research. Let's start with academic research.

Design research is investigative. It's an inquiry into a topic: what it is, what its parts or workings are, its effect on design or on culture. Academic research defines the topic and tells us who has thought about it before. It uncovers primary sources (research about the topic itself) and secondary sources (what others have said about those original researchers' facts or ideas) and shows us where the gaps in our knowledge lie. Who has hated or loved or ignored the subject? Who has made it a life's work? Who has said it should be abandoned, dumped into the nearest dumpster? Since it asks questions, academic research is mainly qualitative. It compares and contrasts the "why and how" of the topic itself or of writing about the topic. This is different from *design research*, which can be a quantitative process, and which I describe a few pages from now in this same chapter.

For designers, the responsibility that comes with academic research can be daunting. First, clear standards have not been established in design in the ways they have been for, say, art history. And second, design students spend far more time in studios than they do mastering aspects of the liberal arts, arts which have spent generations compiling a literature and a heritage of responsibility toward the upholding of academic standards for that literature.

Design as an academic discipline is of mixed heritage: It's both a profession and a field of academic inquiry, and this can be seen as boon or difficulty. In the area of academic research, it's a difficulty. The state of design's academic research is not at the level it could be because students generally have to split their focus between studio and research, and go on to be professionals with split focus or academics with split focus. We are a young area of inquiry, and as such are going through a few awkward years.

Of course, some organizations do uphold high levels of academic rigor—the *Journal of Design History*, for one, and the journal *Visible Language*. The design scholarship coming out of The Royal College of Art, Alvar Aalto University, and the School of Visual Arts all have their academic writing oars firmly planted in the water. And in the Netherlands, the Jan van Eyck Academie and ArtEZ both stress a high level of academic scholarship. But this is only a handful of programs. The United States alone has over 1,600 college-level graphic design programs. And for the average student, the quality, depth, and breadth of academic research are not stressed. When reading student papers or articles, the plight of professors such as I can be summed up in one hair-raising word: Wikipedia.

How to Begin Your Research

When you're assigned an academic research project, the very first thing to do is to make an appointment with the closest librarian. I'll bet your school has a library and that you've only been in it twice, once to find a friend and the other because someone made you take a workshop in its digital lab. You've seen the three books in the glass case outside and you think you know what's going on in there. You might want to revamp your view of what a library is these days.

Librarians are systems-thinkers—they go to school to learn the available systems of knowledge and they can help you shape your inquiry in ways you cannot fathom. If your school has no library, your city does. And all the information available at one is available at the other, thanks to the profound luxury of interwebliness.

The second thing to do when assigned research is to pull out your mind map, your rich club, and any other sketches and ideas you've had for your topic, and let the librarian look through it all. The most important two things the librarian will first tell you are that Google doesn't know everything, and that Wikipedia is not a trustworthy source and is not to be used in bibliographies. Google wants you to think it's indexing everything, but it really isn't—by any stretch of the imagination. In a recent measurement, Google indexed only four percent of what's available on the internet. *Four percent*. Librarians know a number of ways to access the research that Google leaves behind.

Since it's open to collaborative and anonymous editing, Wikipedia is subject to vandals, incorrect facts, and confusions. That said, it has one great use for the beginning of a research quest. When I'm starting an investigation, I often turn to Wikipedia, not to read what it says about a topic, but to scroll down and get to the bibliography. These articles and books are a great resource and a terrific place to start your search. Find those citations and build your first research plans upon them.

While you're researching, don't make the mistake of leaning on listing too many URLs. A list of URLs does not signal sober researching, it betrays a desperate grasping of anything Google listed so as to get the bibliography in on time. To communicate academic gravitas, stick with articles in journals and books. Chances are that you can read them online. Note the book, not the URL. List only a sprinkling of URLs if you want your research to be valued.

A NOTE ON RESEARCH DATABASES

One of the things a librarian can do for you is point you in the direction of subject-appropriate aggregating databases, which are indexes of books and articles from journals that can be searched using keywords, the name of the book, periodical or article, or author. Learning your way around these databases will allow you to make a huge leap in the breadth of your scholarship. Good ones for design scholars currently include: *Art and Architecture Source*, via *EbscoHost*; *Google Scholar*; *JSTOR Arts and Sciences III*; *ProQuest for Design and the Arts*; *Artstor*, for images and information about them; and the *Digital Public Library of America*, which has a searchable collection of over 37,000 images.

As a design student, you may share a number of traits that define excellent researchers: high intelligence, dead honesty, a talent for taking the initiative, a driving curiosity about the world, and perhaps, a tendency toward introversion. For some reason, the best researchers I've known have also had a low-key but wicked sense of humor.[76] If this sounds like you, and if you start to like research and are a bit of a writing nerd, you're positioned well to become a design researcher. This is a job description all its own in the outer world.

THE RULES OF FAIR USE

Now that you've found articles and journals and books and websites that have good material about your topic, how do you use it? Do you just copy and paste chunks of what other people have written into your research? Do you reword another person's ideas and pass them off as your own? No. You do not do these things. The use of work created by others is a complex topic, and you need to know the basics.

For starters, copying and pasting other people's words into your written piece is called *plagiarism*. The word comes from the Latin word *plagiārius*, which means "kidnapper," because you're kidnapping someone's ideas or images. It means stealing. The word first appeared in English in about 1590, so you can see that the problem of people kidnapping other people's stuff has been going on for a while. These days, sadly, we don't hang people for plagiarism. However, being accused of violating someone's copyright can cost you a lot of money, not to mention time, court appearances, and aggravation—ask Shepard Fairey.[77]

If someone uses your language or ideas (or design or photograph) and says that it's their work, the copyright laws protect you. The law considers your words,

---

76 I see that I've just described my former researcher, Sydney Veltcamp.
77 William W. Fisher III et al. "Reflections on the Hope Poster Case," *Harvard Journal of Law and Technology* 25, no. 2 (Spring 2012).

design, and images your legal property. The important thing to remember here is that taking someone's exact words is plagiarism if you don't properly credit them, *but so is rewording someone's idea and passing it off as your own.*

Plagiarism is generally a fault of students willing to compromise their integrity in order to get their paper done; students who think somehow that their teacher is blind to tonal shifts and that plagiarism-spotting tools have not been invented. They forget that if instructors find plagiarism they are contract-bound to report it. So, the plagiarized paper has garnered an instant "F" in the class, and also runs the risk of getting the perpetrator expelled. And it's all so easily avoided.

If you want to use someone's exact words, indent, single space, and quote. If you want to present their ideas without quoting them, reword what they have to say, attribute it to them in the body of your text, and then footnote the document you found it in. This concept, though basic, seems to be foreign to many students, so I include it.

Watch how I handle the next part of this chapter. I'm certainly not inventing pieces of the Copyright Act, but I also don't want to quote huge chunks of a governmental document as an indented quote in my book. So, I *reword and footnote* even though my rewording does not look much like what is written in the original source. It's the *ideas* I'm acknowledging.

You can also reference in other ways. Many forms of academic writing actually discourage footnoting and request text citations—i.e., (Ilyin, 2019)—and a full list of references in the back.

In the United States, use of other people's work is governed by Section 107 of the Copyright Act. This section of the Act explains the four considerations a court uses to decide which ways you can use someone else's work, and which ways you cannot use it. First, they look at the "purpose and character of use, including whether the use is of a commercial nature or is for nonprofit educational purposes."

If you're making a presentation for your class, in school, not profiting financially from the use of images, you most likely fall under the provisions countries make for educational use. The courts generally find that nonprofit educational uses are fair. However, if you use someone else's writing or images in a project that is advertising something like a lecture series for your program or school that will lead to your school collecting money from anyone, don't do it without getting permission from the publisher. Ask yourself, "Will anyone make money from this use?" If so, you need permission.

How are you using the copyrighted work? The court will balance the purpose and character of your use. Is your use "transformative?" Does it add something new, does it cast the subject in a new light? Or is it substituting for the original use of the work? Transformative uses are more likely to be considered "fair use." In the UK this is called "fair dealing."

Second, the court will look at the "nature of the copyrighted work." The court analyzes whether, and to what degree, the work that you used relates to the copyright's purpose of encouraging creative expression. Using something from a novel, a movie, or a song is less likely to support a claim of fair use than using something factual. To restate: The more creative a work is, the more likely the court will find that you stole from it, because the government wants creative people to be encouraged to keep producing.

The third factor in establishing whether what you used was used fairly has to do with the "amount and substantiality of the portion used in relation to the copyrighted work as a whole." The court will look at not only the quality but also the quantity of what you used.

If you decide to include most of a copyrighted work—say, 95 pages of a 100-page novel—the court is unlikely to find that your use was fair. If you only use a small amount of copyrighted material, you have a higher chance of the court ruling fair use. As with so many legal issues, none of this is always true. Sometimes courts have ruled that using an entire work was fair, sometimes they've found that using even a small amount of a copyrighted work was not fair because the selection was at the "heart" of the work.

And the fourth and final test you'll have to pass is the "effect of the use upon the potential market for, or value of, the copyrighted work." Does your use harm the current or future market for the original work? Is your work displacing the sales of the original work? And—this is an interesting criterion: Could your use cause substantial harm if it were to become widespread?

All this to say, be very careful when using other people's work. Every case is different. Unfortunately for us, this means that no clear and specific formula exists—no number of words, for instance—that may be used without permission.[78] Perhaps it all comes down to intent, and to respecting other people's work.

---

78 U.S. Copyright Office, "More Information on Fair Use."Copyright.gov.
    https://www.copyright.gov/fair-use/more-info.html (16 November 2017)

If you're going to make money in some way from the project, and you're worried that what you want to use may cause the hounds of hell to bark upon your doorstep, get permission. Write to the holder of the copyright and ask for permission to use the chunk of the work that you want to use. This may cost you money, particularly if you want to use someone's copyrighted poem or song lyrics.

WHAT *DESIGN* RESEARCH IS AND IS NOT

When I was a young person, my sister Nadia was working toward her degree in chemistry, and I learned from her about research, in particular the technique of knowledge acquisition called the "scientific method." She taught me that this method starts with researchers adopting a *hypothesis*, a statement on what the research will prove about the relationship of two phenomena. They then create a *null hypothesis*, an assertion that there are no grounds for a relationship between their two phenomena.

After that, researchers develop a methodology for testing the null hypothesis against their observations. They measure their findings quantitatively—using numbers to define what's happening—or qualitatively—by describing outcomes. After conducting their experiment and crunching numbers or reviewing outcomes, their findings either prove or disprove the null hypothesis. If it's disproved, the researchers can conclude that there's a relationship between the two phenomena.

Since I had learned about hypotheses when young, that's what I thought research was, because that's what it is in the sciences. So, you can imagine my confusion when I encountered design research for the first time. Gone were the null hypotheses. In fact, I couldn't grasp exactly what *was* going on at first. What was the "right answer" for design research? I saw some researchers looking inward at their own processes. But I also saw designers looking out, observing the ways people lived—the ways they walked to work, or drove, or ferried. These researchers not only observed people, they made educated guesses about their needs and about the ways those needs might be met. They studied, they guessed, and they designed from those guesses.

Then I noticed other kinds of design research. Some design researchers worked out the aesthetics first, prototyped objects or communications, then tested them with prospective users, keeping observational notes on the results of these tests. This whole process was opposite to what the other researchers were doing. These designers guessed, then designed, then tested. Still other designers seemed to be taking social issues and issues of creativity and value into their own hands, testing objects and experiences they created specifically to provoke a critical response in the people who encountered them. These designers wanted to bring their users face-to-face with these questions in order to engage them and provoke awareness of the issues. These researchers designed, then tested, then performed qualitative analysis.

All-in-all, I was confused. With all these different methodologies, what *was* design research? I went looking for a clear explanation, and found these wise words from Trygve Faste, of the Industrial Designers Society of America (IDSA):

> In general, we find that design research approaches tend to fall into one of three categories. Some design research is empirically oriented, based on direct observation of the physical world through qualitative research observing people in context to identify needs and frame opportunities (Faste 1987, Patnaik and Becker 1999, Salvador et al. 1999). Other research focuses on the practice of design as an aesthetically informed form-giving "craft," wherein designers engage in iterative prototyping of forms and experiences to determine their usefulness and usability, often employing field trials and participatory co-design sessions (Smets et al. 1994, Sanders and Stappers 2008). Still others engage in speculative or otherwise theoretical or critical approaches to design that involve systematic probes and interventions into cultural discourse and practice (e.g. Gaver et al. 1999, Dunne and Raby 2001). While each of these activities qualifies as design research, the differences between them can be significant.[79]

Faste reduces the multiplicity of methodologies to three major modes. (Try saying that quickly!) And I finally understood why design research cannot be scientific research. As the makers of the work, designers are an element of their own experiments, so they can't take an exclusively objective approach. They can't create a null hypothesis, because they'd be nullifying themselves. A designer trying to use scientific research methodology would be like the frog in biology class taking notes on the experiment.

This realization was a relief because it made me stop thinking of design research as a lukewarm imitation of scientific research, but as a completely different kind of exploration.

The designer cannot try to prove that something is always true. Design outcomes depend on who the designer is, what the problem is, and for whom the solution is being created. Chemical outcomes do not generally depend on who the chemist is or for whom the solution is being created. But designers' approaches to designing are all different, and every designer must think of the person for whom the solution is being created, or else the experiment fails.

---

79 Trygve Faste, "Demystifying "Design Research," IDSA.org., accessed November 17, 2017, http://www.idsa.org/sites/default/files/Faste.pdf.

The designer looks inward as well as outward. Social scientist Donald Schön has called design "a reflective practice," playing on the meanings of the word "reflect." Designers *reflect* on what they're doing—they think, make and test. Then they *reflect* on the outcomes of the test, and start the process again. They also *reflect* on their work's relationship to the culture, and they *reflect* on the culture around them. They also *reflect* the cultural mores of their time. They're very much a part of the popular cultural system, but they also think deeply about what they find there.

Maarit Mäkelä reminds us that designers understand through making:

> According to Shön, our knowing is in action, ordinarily in tacit form and implicit in our patterns of action. *Reflection-in-Action* indicates a process in which practitioners encounter an unusual situation and have to take a different course of action from that which they usually do or have originally planned.... On the other hand, reflection-on-action includes an analytical process in which practitioners reflect their thinking, actions and feelings in connection to particular events in their professional practice.[80]

Shön's words helped me understand that in order to be valuable, the documentation of design research must show us *reflection in action* and *reflection on action*.

All this I thought through and digested. And from it, here are the elements I believe you should include in the written documentation of your research.

— *Document Observation.*

The current business-speak for this process is "discovery."

First, decide what you want to find out. This may seem basic, but you'd be surprised how often people fail to consider this all-important step.

Second, find people to participate in your research, making sure to have selected an appropriate sample of users. You may be the only observer, or you may recruit observers. (Trained observers are of course best.) Tell participants why you are observing them, what your data will be used for, and how it will not be used.

— *Document Process.*

This allows you and us to reflect on the rigor of your research. For each research project case, begin your documentation immediately, taking notes as you create

---

80 Donald Schön, *The Reflective Practitioner: How Professionals Think in Action*, (New York: Basic Books, 1991), *passim.*

the test problem or project for yourself or for others. Take pictures of everything, keep all scribbled notes, save every sketch. Whether you're looking inside yourself or looking outside at the lives of other people, you will make things in response to the problems you pose. What question did you pose? What did you make? What were the issues you encountered during the making? This is your documentation of reflecting *in action*.[81]

— *Test. Document Test.*

Document what you were testing, what the format of the test was, what you observed, what changed between tests.

— *Compare and Mull.*[82]

Research other experimenters and their outcomes. Document research. How did your testing differ in process and issues encountered?

— *Describe Conclusions.*

After all of the making, testing, and iterations have concluded, review the case. Write what you've learned about your process and about the people for whom you're designing, what you've found out about your own practice or about their needs as a result of the research, and detail how the research has altered or changed your practice or the experience of your test subjects. This is reflecting *on action*.

To document your research successfully, reflect "in and on action," going back and forth between the two as you explain your ideas and the details of their testing. Adopt a professional tone and a slightly formal style, lean on ethos and logos as your persuading methods, try diagramming with tree and caravan arguments, and conclude with remarks about the value of the research to you and to us.

What Is the Peer Review Process?

If you become an academic, and particularly if you want to publish in scientific or academic journals, your paper or article may be subject to a formal process

---

81 Robert Baxter, this book's designer, likes to use a technique in scientific documentation as a guiding principle for documenting process: In the physical sciences and in mathematics, the logbook is the equivalent process document, and it has two shining never-broken rules: 1. Everything goes into the logbook, and 2. Nothing in the logbook can be destroyed—if you make a mistake, you strike it out, but it is still readable. In this way he builds a very interesting narrative of process.

82 When I worked for her, Caroline Hightower, a former executive director of the AIGA, described the creative process as, "Mull, mull, mull—*Voilá!*" Once you've done your testing and research, you must give yourself time to mull over these inputs so that your creative unconscious can spit out ideas your logical mental processes have not yet understood.

called peer review. Peer review is exactly that—review by people deemed your peers in your field of expertise. Highly structured, the process helps publishers decide whether your work is valid and has value in the larger conversation about your topic.

You can see why publishers would want to review your work this way—they're publishers, not scientists or designers, and they know they cannot ascertain the quality or originality of work not in their area of expertise. Publishers also believe that knowing their work will undergo peer review makes writers more careful, filters out poor work, keeps standards of inquiry high, and maintains the house's reputation.

The process of Peer Review generally follows this format:

— 1   An author submits a paper. The editorial office checks the paper against the journal's guidelines to make sure it's formatted according to its requirements for organization and style. No one looks at the quality of the work yet.

— 2   Next, the editor-in-chief gives the paper a short review, making sure it's right for the journal and that it seems interesting and worthy of continuing the process. If not, the editor rejects it. If the paper makes it past the editor-in-chief, it's assigned to an associate editor, who becomes the "handling editor" of the piece's journey through the peer review process. This editor then invites people to be reviewers, and continues inviting people until receiving the required number of acceptances. This required number varies with each publisher.

— 3   The reviewers read the paper several times—first, to get a preliminary impression. If that first impression is bad, the reviewer rejects the paper and notifies the publisher. If that impression is good, the reviewer reads the paper more times, taking review notes. Then the reviewer sends back the manuscript and notes to the journal, together with a recommendation to accept or reject it—or to have the author revise it. The handling editor considers the reviews, makes a decision about whether to publish the piece or ask for revisions, and communicates with the author. If the paper is sent back for revision, the reviewers will see it again after revisions have been made and submitted.

Submitting your work for peer review can feel awkward at first, just as though you're sitting in hospital gown while a team of doctors poke and prod. But it's a wonderful time to practice your breathing, work on reducing your ego's grasp, and open up your ears to critical appraisal.

CHAPTER ELEVEN

Writing Long
Bibliographies, Research Papers,
& Master's Theses

W E'VE SUDDENLY ARRIVED AT LONG-FORM ACADEMIC WRITING. When I think that just a few pages ago I was talking about bundles of meaningful marks and describing how to sit down at the writing table and let your ideas unfold—well, my eyes get misty with remembrance, and I long for the simplicity of those far-off days.

We've already covered much of what you need to know about writing long—researching, diagramming, and structuring arguments; figuring out which persuasive mode to use and which tone and voice; the writing of complex think pieces and shorter critical pieces—all of these are in the pages behind this one. If you're just dipping into the book to find out about how to do one of these things, go to the index and hunt those pages down. If you're at this chapter after completing all other chapters, I'm willing to bet you're at a fairly high level of writing proficiency at this point, and ready for a bit of a change. So, let's start with bibliographies.

Invisible Argument:
The Art of the Annotated Bibliography

A couple of years ago, after many terms of requiring research papers from our "Critical and Contextual Thinking" undergraduates, Liz[83] and I suddenly had had enough of the reading of papers. We decided to take a break from them while requiring more of the students, which is a nice little trick to pull off, I must say.

I remembered that, back in my grad school days, I had come upon a series of wonderful annotated bibliographies created by Andrew Blauvelt, then teaching in North Carolina and now director of the Cranbrook Art Museum in Michigan. These annotated bibliographies, bibliographies with short notes about each citation, detailed the books and articles particular to studying various design and cultural studies subjects. I found them invaluable when I was in grad school. In one grand gesture, Blauvelt had mapped most of the books and articles read or mentioned in the graduate education of that era. That meant that I—in my overwhelmed state—didn't have to find and contextualize all these books and articles. He'd found them for me. I just had to read them.[84]

This memory of the Blauvelt bibliographies coincided with our concern that design history texts did not paint an inclusive picture of the story of design. So, Liz and I decided to ask our students to create annotated bibliographies instead of term research papers. These bibliographies, about a person or group they felt had been left out of design history texts, were to contain 80 to 100 citations, all of them with fifty-word annotations that described what the book or article was about and why it was appropriate for inclusion in the study of design history for future researchers.

Finding 80 to 100 books, articles, and websites about a little-known person or group and writing 80 to 100 "notes-to-future-researchers" about these citations is a lot of work. But the students pulled it off like champs. And, after doing all that research, some of them asked to write up their findings in paper form. Stunned, I believe we allowed them to do so. Once you've done so much research, it really is tempting to write about it. What a switch of consciousness.

---

83 Elisabeth Patterson co-teaches design history and criticism with me at Cornish College of the Arts in Seattle. She's a true teacher, and an inspiring colleague and co-conspirator.

84 When reading large numbers of texts, as you must in grad school, make sure to use your grad school reading technique, described much earlier in this book. Read the first line of each paragraph of the entire text to get the shape of the argument, marking those that seem important to your research, then go back to the marked paragraphs and read those.

If you're an instructor, I very much recommend mixing it up with an "annotated bibliography instead of a paper" assignment every few terms. Of course, as will become clear, I am also a proponent of research papers, and I make a case for them a few pages from now. But the annotated bibliography is a great way for systems-thinking designers to map a lot of information relatively quickly, and the skill translates well to their future design practice, so it has a special value in their education.

IF YOU'VE JUST BEEN ASSIGNED AN
ANNOTATED BIBLIOGRAPHY

First, do not avoid the assignment. Immediately follow the guidelines in the section on academic research in this book. If you have even a hazy area of interest in mind, a librarian can help you focus your ideas and show you the research tools available at your institution.

Second, divide the number of annotations by the number of weeks left until the deadline, with a few days of padding, and research and add that many annotations per week to your research. If your deadline is eleven weeks away and you need 80 to 100 citations, you need to find and annotate approximately nine citations a week. Get started now so that you don't get into a big pile-up at the end of the term. This is one project that you cannot create at the last minute because you need to write those annotations.

When writing annotations, do not plagiarize, i.e., don't just take a few words from the introduction of the book and pretend you wrote them. It's so tempting to just quote a little something and not attribute it, but stealing is a very bad idea. Big consequences. If you want to use that piece of the introduction, or someone else's writing, put it in quotes and footnote. See the plagiarism section if you're confused. *If you want to restate something an author has said, you still need to note or reference.* But your bibliography will carry more weight if you figure out what's in the book and then give us the gist in two or three sentences of your own words. Write as though you're writing to a grad student who's looking for material in your area. Giving us the "who, what, when, where, why" of the publication. That's all.

The interesting thing here is that, though they look terribly objective, bibliographies are malleable systems and can be as biased and subjective as anything else can be. By choosing what you put in and what you leave out, you're nudging your reader towards your point of view, even though you don't seem to be writing anything that's trying to convince. As you write your annotations, stick with ethos and logos. I have yet to read a heart-wrenching bibliography, pathos not being the career academic's best move. But now that I think of it, if Nabokov can write a whole novel as though it were a poem and commentary, perhaps you can write one that masquerades as an annotated bibliography.[85]

EXERCISE FIFTEEN
Build an Annotated Bibliography

Create a twenty-citation annotated bibliography using the Chicago Style method of notation. As you find citations, create a nodal map of the information you uncover. Map different ways the works show relationship. Who are the main actors? What are the main topics these people pondered? What personal and thematic relationships become apparent in your nodal map? This organizing will help you find ways to group the material that will exert a subtle influence on the way the user experiences the topic. Can you use this bibliographical work to build a part of a project you've been assigned in another class? If another project is not available, research your favorite contemporary African designer. "Contemporary" meaning working in the last ten years.

In Defense of the Term Paper

For design students, the dreaded *term paper* rarely rears its head. There's a current trend away from requiring such draconian assignments in design history and criticism. "When will they ever use these skills again?" ask writing and history teachers. "Let's give them something more pragmatic, like blogging."

Design writing and history instructors are a generally tough breed, and think nothing of requiring impossibly big and complex projects to be done in short amounts of time. But they too have their weaknesses: Having to read and correct seventy-five or so thirty-page term papers is punishment beyond endurance for even the most hardened of the lot. So, between your design writing instructors' wanting to make your experience more useful and your history teachers'

---

85 Some people consider Nabokov's *Pale Fire* to be his greatest novel. It's written as a poem and its critical commentary, but, read together, the pieces create a novel in the mind of the reader.

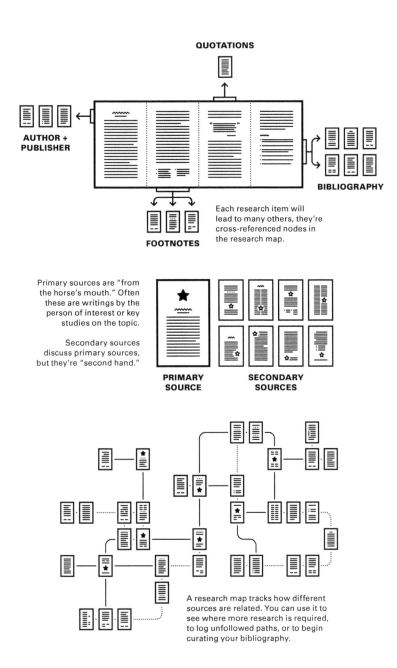

QUOTATIONS

AUTHOR + PUBLISHER

BIBLIOGRAPHY

Each research item will lead to many others, they're cross-referenced nodes in the research map.

FOOTNOTES

Primary sources are "from the horse's mouth." Often these are writings by the person of interest or key studies on the topic.

Secondary sources discuss primary sources, but they're "second hand."

PRIMARY SOURCE

SECONDARY SOURCES

A research map tracks how different sources are related. You can use it to see where more research is required, to log unfollowed paths, or to begin curating your bibliography.

fig 11.1

A bibliography is a curated map of information. The researcher/writer surveys the terrain and determines which landmarks and small mountains and overgrown paths will be important for later researchers.

exhaustion with the day-to-day of academic existence, you're not getting a lot of practice writing long.

True, no instructor should ever be sentenced to reading thirty pages of the rephrased Wikipedia mash-up that passes for research paper-writing in many institutions today.

Much better for your instructor to assign a designed poster with the facts about William Morris or Charles and Ray Eames on the reverse and be done with it, if writing is not currently championed in your institution.

But writing research papers—and this is what I mean when I say "term papers"—is a skill worth having. I mean really *writing* them. I mean mind mapping, nodal mapping, rich club diagramming, researching, drafting, and writing. I mean the whole shebang. And the reason I feel this set of skills is valuable for you, even if you think you'll never use research skills again, is exactly that: You may never again have the opportunity to think through, research, and write such a piece of your own scholarship.

You may never get to be the person in the world that knows more than anyone else knows about something. Not in the "Google" sense: In the deep-thinking sense. You may very well write more genuine scholarship about the subject than any other design academic ever has. Design is a young discipline, and its scholarship is a very young scholarship. There's plenty of room for students to add to the conversation. Thinking about one subject for a whole term is an unheard of luxury of thought, and only in the academy do people have the time to think things through as completely. Long writing uses a part of the brain that Twitter does not. It is thought as symphony, not as blurt. Writing scholarship provides a unique opportunity for self-enrichment, and it goes a long way toward disrupting the homogenization of human experience toward which much technological advance seems to be leading.

There's an attitude in education administration right now that champions entertaining students. These administrators believe that making things more entertaining keeps students from getting bored, keeps them "engaged," and, most important, keeps them enrolled. Because you may have grown up with gaming and bashing and zooming, these administrators imagine that gaming and bashing and zooming is the only kind of thinking that you want to do. I think administrators will look back on this strategy in a few years and see its shortcomings clearly.

When you're a student, there's something crucial about putting yourself in a difficult place and battling through to the other side, doing something really hard that tests the limits of who you thought you were, that builds the self-esteem and resilience you will need to survive life. It is only through meeting appropriate challenges that you become really confident: Only through challenging yourself do you begin to pat around the walls of your identity and find the shape of your own abilities—only through challenge that you build the courage to fill that shape out.

Here's the thing: *My students don't seem to desire entertainment.* Though they may start out—as many do—telling me that they hate to read, that history or criticism is too dry a subject for them, that instructors don't understand who they are or appreciate their special personal needs, I find that all of this goes away pretty fast when that student experiences triumph over a hard challenge in a safe place.

A real student is a person who seeks out difficult spots in order to figure out how to get out of those spots. Showing up to do something you've never done is a hard spot. Writing a real, well-written research paper is a hard spot. You're an educated person when you make the creation and negotiation of hard spots a part of your identity. In the same way that a mended hairline fracture strengthens bone, small, negotiable threats to your world view—or to your view of your own abilities—builds your confidence and resilience. Creating a research paper is a negotiable threat. Intellectual resilience is the edge that an educated person has in the world. It's the only lasting thing that school can give you.

Admittedly, "writing long" is an arduous process. But when you write a research paper, you're setting yourself up not to fear whatever the written component of your BFA will be. You're preparing yourself not to agonize over the written component of your MFA thesis. "Fifty pages? Is that all? I researched and wrote thirty in college!" That's what you want to hear your subconscious saying when you see the requirements for your MFA. You'll be ready when someone at your new job wants you to do professional research. You'll know how to assemble research, how to sort through it, and how to find the valuable bits and pieces.

Structuring and Writing Research Papers

Writing an academic research paper is a bit different from writing a "complex think piece" because you're not leading with an idea of your own, making it the focal point, and convincing your reader of its worth. The successful academic research paper is exactly what it says it is: It's a survey or summary of what's out there about your chosen topic, with your comments added along the way.

You aren't comparing someone's work to what you think it should be. That's criticism. Your success depends on how well you synthesize the ideas of others. True, you might scatter moments of your own warmly-hued brilliance along the way—but these small nuggets are thoughts you have had while comparing or contrasting other people's work. Your job is to find and map the sources valuable to your exploration, synthesize them, and make remarks that bind one to the next. These remarks center on ideas you've had while doing the research, such as relationships you've found of one source to another or quirky notions you've uncovered as you've thought and synthesized.

What does "synthesize" mean in this context? It means boiling your research down to each source's essential ideas and then relating those ideas to one another in fresh and appealing ways. You're the person responsible for the "fresh and appealing" part.

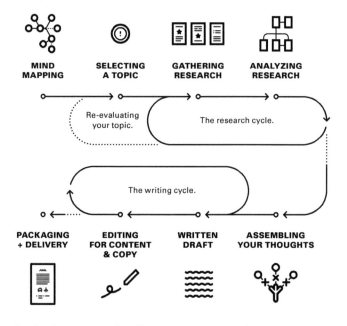

MIND MAPPING **SELECTING A TOPIC** **GATHERING RESEARCH** **ANALYZING RESEARCH**

Re-evaluating your topic.

The research cycle.

The writing cycle.

PACKAGING + DELIVERY **EDITING FOR CONTENT & COPY** **WRITTEN DRAFT** **ASSEMBLING YOUR THOUGHTS**

fig 11.2

A research paper process iteration feedback loop.

Most kinds of writing can handle a certain amount of procrastination on the part of the writer. We all know people who "avoid to control," and, on the night before the project is due—cortisol pumping—spit out a ten-page paper and then collapse. "Sprints," said a character in the film *Chariots of Fire*, "are for neurotics."

No one can dash 26.219 miles. To write serious research, you must think like a marathoner, start prepping weeks in advance of the actual event, and adopt a pace that you can maintain for the duration of the race.

Break the project down into stages. Put these stages in your calendar, working backwards from a week before your due date. (Every schedule needs "air," or flexibility. You'll be sure to come down with a cold at some point.) The first stages of this process are: mind mapping, selecting a topic, gathering research, sorting research, diagramming research, and finding the rich club in your research nodes. These stages form a feedback loop and can go on for days or weeks, depending on your deadline.

The next stages are: synthesizing research, drafting your thoughts about the research, assembling these thoughts, writing a first draft, editing for content, writing a second draft, copyediting, attaching illustrations and appended information, tying with a large bow, and presenting to professor.

EXERCISE SIXTEEN
Create a "Process Machine"

Clearly, you're not going to write a research paper here. But select a topic—perhaps one that's been required in another class—and, after selecting this topic, make a circular diagram to guide you through the stages of the process: mind mapping, finding the rich club, gathering research, sorting research, diagramming research. This diagram is your "process machine." It's a feedback loop that allows you to add information through the weeks, constantly organizing and questioning. This working process document contains all your research and ideas as diagram and notes.

THE DESIGN MASTER'S THESIS:
I HEAR A SYMPHONY

In design, a master's thesis generally requires three things: a body of work made around a particular idea or topic; a written component that combines a complex think piece with notes on process; and a thesis document, into which both of the former are poured. (Though these are generally required, every school's requirements differ, so do read the guidelines your program gives you and adjust accordingly.) The parameters of this book demand that I focus on the written part of this symphony of making. So, in the written component, plan to include:

— 1   An "abstract," or short overview of your exploration
        (I'd go tree. Make it tight as a drum. No wandering.)

— 2   Introduction (tree?)

— 3   Expository Essay (house?)

— 4   Documenting the Work (caravan?)

— 5   Discussion of Aesthetics, Technique or Method (included in above)

— 6   Sources (Keep that bibliography up-to-date through the process.)

— 7   Conclusion

As you scout around, mind mapping and playing with finding nodes of content, beginning to tighten the lariat on the ideas you want to explore, put it all down in writing. Take notes on all the exercises and small projects you do (or have done) during your graduate work that will fit into your thesis exploration. Include both the successful experiments and the duds.

Here's a trick. When you get to an idea you think will hold up as a thesis, draft a rough introductory paragraph and a rough concluding paragraph for the text of your written component. (This will relieve some stress. These paragraphs will both change many times, but you'll work in a less constricted manner because you'll know you have something down for a beginning and an end, and the middle of the sandwich will be all you need to fill in.)

Early in the term, visit a librarian and show all your mapping and diagramming of what you're thinking about. Although the written component of the thesis is primarily a complex think piece—your own research and thinking—you'll be exploring the thoughts that other people have had about the topics you unearth. The written component includes academic research, your own expository writing, and thoughts you've synthesized from your making and exploration.

After mind mapping and creating a rich club of topics and ideas and drafting a first and last paragraph, create a working diagram of a plausible narrative arc for the entire piece. Then fill in bits and pieces as you experiment with your making and have ideas about the things you make. Update your introduction and conclusion paragraphs as your ideas change. Schedule structured time every day for noodling around, updating your paragraphs and diagrams, and reviewing your rich club thinking.

If you do these things, you'll have an evolving manuscript, in process from the beginning, written as you go along. Keeping this document going means you won't have to look ahead to that dark and terrible day when you'll *have to start writing*. You'll have already started writing from Day One, and you will have thought about your ideas and making over and over, and edited your written bits and pieces over and over. They'll be in a reasonable order, smoothed out, and cleaned up by the time you're ready to start designing your thesis document.

From the first minute of the first day of grad school, put a notebook by your computer and scribble bits and pieces of ideas about possible thesis questions as you have them. When you officially start your thesis project, adopt a three-part writing process: *Have design idea, develop idea, make. Write thoughts about idea and outcomes of experimentation in notebook.* Never design without a notebook moment. Think of it as a break from the screen.

Don't forget that *an important element of the thesis process is the restricted time in which you must complete it.*[86] It's good to remember that all this writing and making may map out the work of many future years, but the thesis itself must form a complete project in just a few months.

When not engaged in making work, note down things like: thoughts on your original thesis statement, backing up that statement, poking holes in it, wondering who else has thought about it, documenting those people, and agreeing or disagreeing with their ideas. This kind of discursive work, included finally in the written component, will make your writing rich and satisfying to those professorial souls who must read it.

EXERCISE SEVENTEEN
Three Basic Questions

These might help you focus on the one topic you want to explore for your project.

After spending five minutes getting into your writing, spend about fifteen minutes on each of the following questions.

---

86 My friend Matthew Monk shared these immortal words with me when I was embroiled in my own thesis.

— 1 In one sentence, tell me who you are. (Admittedly, this is a terribly hard question. But do it first. Students often say they look back at this question as snapping things into focus for them.)

— 2 If you had one chance to tell every designer in the world one thing, what would that one thing be?

— 3 If you had time and resources to create only one thing (no worrying about money or practicalities in this dreamscape) and this was the only thing you'd ever be able to make, what would this thing be?

Spend five minutes coming out of your writing, then sit back and see what you've said. Where do your thoughts about self and meaning send you? Take notes.

EXERCISE EIGHTEEN
Getting to a Thesis Statement

When you're ready, try this next set of questions. Spend five minutes going into your writing. Then answer these at your own pace.

— 1 What is the question your thesis will answer? (This is your elevator pitch: one sentence that describes your group of interests.)

— 2 Why do you want to make work about this question? (This is where you put the stories about how you were led to this interest.)

— 3 How do these ideas help build the design conversation, make it larger, or more inclusive?

— 4 For what audience are you making this project, and why should anyone care about it? (Get specific.)

— 5 Who will be affected by your project?
(Beyond your audience at the exhibition, who is your practical audience? Who will use what you design?)

— 6 How will your thesis be remembered and retold?[87]

---

87 I've been using and modifying these questions for years, but I believe Anne West first asked them of me.

Your faculty will give you specific proposal guidelines, but the questions above may help you focus your ideas so that you can write their requested proposal with a minimum of stress, according to their specifications.

If you have answered all the questions sincerely, reviewed your thoughts with faculty and respected peers, thought about their reactions (making changes in your approach that you feel need to be made after these conversations), and fitted the material to your school's specifications, you're well on your way to a solid thesis proposal.

I enjoyed talking about papers and theses. But let us now wend our way down from the sparkling crest of the academic mountain, and commingle our tracks once again in the village snow of everyday design writing.

CHAPTER TWELVE

Writing to People

WE INHABIT A COMMUNICATIVE WORLD OF TWEETS AND INSTAGRAM, but sometimes—to get an internship or find a job—you'll need to write a more formal, longer email to someone you don't know. If you're not used to talking to strangers, this can stop you cold. It's not the writing itself that can be daunting, it's the idea of making a fool of yourself by asking for something and getting rejected, coupled with the queasy feeling that knocking on the private world of an unknown person and demanding entrance is somehow inappropriate, even in these days of everyone's overexposure.

But think of it this way. Writing to people is an act of imagination. Whether business email or love note, you create a tiny world in your head every time you prompt a conversation with someone you don't know. Imagine what you want to have happen—really imagine it. Close your eyes and imagine trading banter with colleagues at the internship or digging into a project at the desk of your new job. Now imagine that you already know the person you're writing to, though not well. Now write that note.

In Admiration

Sometimes, when I'm sorting out the built-up junk mail in my design office mailbox, I come across a little envelope with handwriting on it. When I open it, it's from some kind person who read something I wrote and just wanted to tell me something about it. It's not a long note, but I read every word twice, feel my hunched shoulders begin to straighten, and start saying chirpy things around the office, hoping someone will notice the envelope in my hand and ask what it is.

A note like that can change a person's trajectory. Although we all do the usual social media things and appreciate the positive things said there, absolutely nothing compares to a note in the faculty mailbox. The person had to find pen and paper and stamp—and then spent time to write a kind word. Writers spend much of their careers tapping on the wall of a solitary cell. They get used to doing the tapping and don't really expect someone to tap back. Imagine what it feels like when someone does. If you get a note like this, respond. "The great write back," said my wonderful professor, Sr. Nicholas Maltman, O.P.

Barriers to writing to someone you don't know can be hard to jump. So, let's start by getting out paper, an envelope and a stamp, and writing the least threatening letter there is: a letter of admiration.

EXERCISE NINETEEN
Write a Note

Write a note to a designer or writer you admire. Just write it by hand, no need to make it a designed object, unless you want to do so.

What to say?

Start with "Dear X," ("Dear" is still used in letters—I wouldn't use a "Dear" in an email, but I do use it in letters). Then pull out your journalist's standbys, "who, what, when, where, and why."

Say who you are, say what this person's work has meant to you, or what particular thing they've made that you've appreciated, or what you'd like to ask them about something they said. Tell them when you found their work or when you realized it was important to you. Tell where it has taken you emotionally or intellectually, and explain why.

It's not a business letter. You don't have to use a formal "close." Just sign it. Find the person's studio or company address. Buy a stamp. (Buy a few while you're at it. Keep them in your wallet for the next time you decide to write a letter of admiration.) Address and stamp the note. Put the note in a mailbox.

BECAUSE YOU WANT SOMETHING—LIKE A JOB

When I taught seniors, I would assign them the task of writing emails to two designers they didn't know, to ask them to act as mentors for their final BFA project. I still remember one student—ordinarily a very calm and hipster-type of person—sitting in front of his computer, the perspiration pouring off of him as he wrote to an art director he admired. Imagine his delight when that art director wrote back immediately. Imagine my delight that they work together now.

Students don't generally mind writing a physical letter of admiration. But the works start to gum up when they need to ask someone they don't know for something they really want.

Here are the important things to remember when you write an email to a person you do not know.

— *Be clear and direct.*

Everyone is busy. Don't spend a long time clearing your throat. Remember how you wrote the admiring letter above? Adopt that tone. And adopt that brevity.

— *Talk more about them, less about you.*

Often students feel they must write a paragraph about their career goals and education right up front in the email, so that the person they're writing to will take them seriously and give their request some thought. Do not do this. After the briefest one-sentence introduction of yourself, avoid talking about your own goals and desires. Remember the tone of the fan note. Talk about the person or company to which you're writing.

— *Stick with who, what, when, where, how, and why.*

Perhaps not in that order. After you tell who you are—in one sentence, tell why you're writing. What do you admire about this person's work or studio? How can your skills support the studio's objectives? When will be convenient to meet briefly? Where? Thank them for their consideration. Make the writing short, intelligent, and clear.

— *Avoid being too formal or too informal.*

Use the language you would use when talking with your slightly older co-worker or a young faculty member. Warm, but not familiar. Informal, but not too casual. Look at the section on tone in this book (Chapter 9) if you need to brush up.

— *Get in, make your pitch, and get out.*

Introduce yourself, ask for what you want, tell them you'll check back in, and sign off politely. The "check back in" part is crucial: It gives you a reason to write back and nudge them.

— No guts, no glory.

It's very hard to ask for something you really want. But think of the universe as one of those huge soap bubbles you see people making in parks. Then imagine you're inside an enormous one. If you give the wall of the bubble a little push, you can see the force of your energy tremble through the walls—watch the bubble change shape slightly or move onto a slightly new course. That energy transfer happens every time you push for something you want. Every time you direct your energy in a focused way, you change the shape of the future. Apply for that internship you'd love to get or that job you'd love to have. Over time, the force of little pushes changes everything.

EXERCISE TWENTY
Write a Convincing Email

Write an email to a designer you admire asking for something you really want.

Use the tone of the note you wrote for the "letter of admiration."

Explain who you are, why you value their work, a particular thing you've liked or what you'd like to ask them about something they said, tell why you're writing, say when you'll contact them again if you don't hear from them, and sign off.

Avoid using the truncation, "Best" as a closing. It comes from "Best regards," or "Best wishes." Should you want to send regards or wishes, by all means send them. But don't send a lonesome "Best."

Check and recheck the spelling of everything. I've decided not to hire people on the strength of spelling alone. It shows a lack of attention to detail.

Do a little dance for luck, and hit that send button.

BECAUSE YOU DON'T WANT SOMETHING—LIKE A CLIENT

There will come a moment in your designer-life when it's time to fire a client. Generally, the moment doesn't happen because of crazy behavior on anyone's part. All design has fraught client relationships. No, it usually happens because your work has changed course, but you still have a client from days gone by hanging on, who is billed only a fraction of your current billing rate, yet who expects full

136

service because of the longevity of the relationship. Much as you love to reminisce about the good old days, at some point dear old Joe has got to go.

But how do you do it? Of course, a personal conversation is best. But if you're concerned that you'll get swayed by Joe's sad and lonesome look when you break the news, write an email.

— *Be clear and direct.*

As in other correspondence, be clear and direct. Again, don't spend a long time clearing your throat. Odd as it sounds, be positive. Not a cheerleader, not too upbeat, but not overly apologetic or negative. Reference the fan letter above. Adopt that tone, and adopt that brevity.

— *Talk more about them, less about you.*

After the briefest one sentence introduction that explains the ways your business has changed, bring the subject back to them. What are their plans for the future? How do they foresee their business developing? Who would be a good fit going forward? This may seem antithetical, but it reframes the conversation. Don't butter Joe up. Just be appreciative of the past and clear about the future.

— *Stick with who, what, when, where, how, and why.*

Again, not in that order. Tell Joe how the company has changed direction—in one sentence. Explain why you're writing. How can you support their finding a designer more suited to their current needs? Be positive, not dirge-like.

— *Avoid being too formal or too informal.*

Again, use the language you would use when talking with your slightly older co-worker or a young faculty member. Warm, but not familiar. Informal, but not casual.

— *No guts, no glory, again.*

It's very hard to put your ego on the line and ask for something you really want—in this case, freedom. But do it for Joe. You may be using Joe as an insurance policy. "If everything collapses, we still have Joe." Not a great way to treat Joe. Sweep away the cobwebs, give the client a fresh start somewhere else, and put all your energy into your business's current direction.

Write a Client-Firing Email

Use the tone of the note you wrote for the "letter of admiration."

Choose Logos or Ethos as your form of persuasion. Pathos is a bit much.

Explain the direction your company is going, tell why you value your past work together, tell them you're ending the relationship, ask when's a good time to meet to abrogate the contracts in person (if this is necessary) and sign off.

Check and recheck spelling.

Do another little dance, this time, of celebration, and hit that send button.

Generally, remember to write emails as if someone other than the recipient is reading them; avoid sarcasm or anything that would embarrass you if it was read out loud in a meeting.

LETTERS ON PAPER

I've been trying to remember the last letter I received in the mail. I believe it was a contractual letter from my provost. And months before that, I think I got a note from a friend who writes notes because she doesn't want her confidences flying around, loose in electrons. She's a lawyer, so she's often reminded me that mail tampering is illegal, but monitoring someone's emails is not. So, the mails really are still the most private form of correspondence.

Although email has replaced almost all business correspondence, important contracts—like design contracts and book contracts—are still often sent via post/mail. And any time you have to deal with anything legal, actual letters are still the best way to communicate. So, let's run through the basics.

I'm imagining that you know the parts of a physical business letter. They are the heading—your name, return address, and date—the sender's address, the salutation, the body, the closing, and the signature. The salutation for most formal physical letters is "Dear Mr. or Ms. X." Alternatively, you can write "Dear Joe Smith," if you don't want to call out gender. For the body of the letter, follow the suggestions for the body of an email, above.

For legal matters, use a formal tone (see the discussion on tone in Chapter 9) and, if you must argue a point, stick to tree arguments. Legal letters are not the place for digression. Use "what, when, where, why, and how" directness, and be completely factual: Include names, dates, and pertinent data.

Closings can be tricky. The current "Best," feels vague and truncated at the same time. These days I've gone back to "Sincerely" in letters, since it means I am being sincere, which, in a legal contract, I am undoubtedly being.

Although you may currently send letters that contain proposals and contracts, I also suggest that you either begin or sharpen your skills at writing love letters. This suggestion is entirely practical: Both love and the post office need support these days. Writing love letters is an excellent practice. It will remind you of your being human. It will also leave a physical track of your time on the planet, should you not be in the book publishing business.

I have some letters my great-great grandfather sent to my great-great grandmother in the 1890's, before he was killed in a gunfight in Texas. I know who he was because of those letters; I know who she was. I know their everyday problems were a lot like my everyday problems. I know they loved each other. And when I look at those letters, I'm reminded how similar all human lives really are.

Your progeny will not be looking through your thousands of emails to find that little spate of correspondence you had with their grandmother way back in 2025. Email will be long gone. But love letters on paper have a funny way of surviving. They remind us of our context, of our value, of our connectedness to other people, no matter whether those people are living or dead. In our time, writing and mailing a love letter is a radical and truly private act. No one is reading over your shoulder. Make sure to get the address right and put a stamp on it.[88]

---

88 This said, it's important not to just talk about yourself in love letters. Love makes narcissists of us all, but focus the letter on the person to whom you're writing. And be careful about introducing subject matter aside from the beloved. Long ago, my delight in receiving a note from a paramour faded rapidly when it turned out to be a long letter about how he had fixed a toilet.

CHAPTER THIRTEEN

Business Proposals & Reports

WHEN WRITING PROPOSALS AND REPORTS, remember that the person who reads your work will have very little time to do so. I keep a little sketch of a clock posted to my computer screen to remind myself not to spend the client's time being vague or wordy. The facts need to be right there and the voice—the voice of your design office—must be identifiably yours. The most successful proposals and reports are clear and direct, with a formal structure and slightly less formal, warm tone.

A WORD ON BUSINESS-SPEAK

As a writer, I dislike jargon of most kinds, and counsel you to avoid using buzzwords. A few years ago, I had a fairly public outburst in *Metropolis* magazine about designers using the word "passion" to describe the ardor they feel for their work. The word "passion" has its roots in the word "suffering." People at that time were evidently suffering all over the place because of their attachment to graphic design. Thank heavens the passion seems to have simmered down, but now designers are transforming, innovating, crafting, seizing, nurturing, and "advancing the human experience." No wonder we're tired. Perhaps we should wear climbing-wall shoes to work, since we're evidently the Spidermen of the business community. These words are buzzwords. Use your ears. If you've heard an expression at the last three meetings, avoid it. Write business the way you speak business. The less hype the better.

A SIMPLE PROPOSAL FOR GETTING NEW BUSINESS

Proposals are an art in themselves. Some are big and require that you put a rather complex system in place to create them, but some are relatively small and direct. When you're first starting out as a freelancer, it's unlikely that you'll be filing responses to requests for proposals (RFPs; see below). But you will have clients large and small, and those clients will want to hear about how you plan to approach their project, what the timeline will be (because they need it right now), and how much it will cost.

Most designers have found or created a template for their proposal writing. They write one, or get it written, then spend the next few years changing the names and a few of the details and the estimates and sending the same proposal out to clients. This seems a rather canned response, and although it gets a proposal to the client quickly—which has value—it doesn't give you an opportunity to focus the proposal on the client in a way that will be persuasive (see Chapter 8: Convincing). And since you're evidently a transforming, innovating, crafting, seizing, nurturing, and advancing "the human experience" kind of person, perhaps you'd like to think about proposal writing as a project, rather than as paperwork. Think about a client you'd love to have, and write a dummy proposal. Play around with diagramming a simple proposal "kit of parts":

— 1   What We Understand About You (the Client)

— 2   What We Understand About Your Project

— 3   What We Recommend

— 4   A Project Schedule

— 5   Projected Estimates and Costs

— 6   Who We Are

— 7   Case Studies and References

Make a diagram and write a draft first, before doing any web research about how other designers write proposals. Let your mind have free rein, and just explain each point as if you were talking to an intelligent colleague. No buzzwords. Once you have a draft in your own voice, you can research and see what other people do about proposals. There's no "right answer" with a proposal, as long as you make clear what you believe the project is, what your proposed time frame is, what the proposed schedule is, what the numbers are, and what you plan to do for that money. If you add in anything from what you find in the research, make sure it doesn't transform, innovate, craft, seize, nurture, or advance anything but your real voice.

Map, Diagram, & Write a Simple Proposal

Imagine that an old acquaintance has just asked you to design a logo, a menu and front
window sign for her new motorcycle-themed macaroni restaurant. Create a proposal
using the technique and steps outlined above.

RESPONDING TO THE REQUEST FOR PROPOSAL

An RFP is a "Request for Proposal." Institutions like schools, governmental offices,
and large companies generally send them out because they have the resources to
spend staff time on finding a designer from a large pool of candidates and because
they must make it clear that they are conducting a transparent search, and that
they aren't hiring someone's brother-in-law. These organizations also use the RFP
to streamline the process of deciding on whom they plan to hire and so require
that you answer specific questions and give specific information about the ways
you plan to handle the project.

Generally, these are relatively large projects, and will require that you form a
team in order to get the job done. You will describe each person on that team in
the response to the RFP, so start rustling up those people's bios. Here are the parts
of a response to a typical RFP:

— 1   Background (What We Understand About Your Project)

— 2   (Our Design Firm's) Design Recommendations

— 3   Our Design Development Schedule

— 4   Our Project Schedule

— 5   Estimates and Costs (Projected)

— 6   Statement of Capability (Description of Company and Team Bios)

— 7   Case Studies (Annotated Portfolio Pieces Detailing Process)

— 8   References

— 9   Terms and Conditions

These bits and pieces will move around according to the client, but all RFPs include all of this information.

Submitting a response to an RFP is a more formal process than submitting a simple proposal. Get it in by the due date, keep the writing clear, and remember that the team that is reviewing your response will be confronted with a large pile of actual or PDF responses. So, don't waste their time with puff, exaggeration, or being vague. If asked for a physical proposal, design it simply, don't put in any over-designed or clever pieces that will fall out or get lost or use any unusual binding that will damage other proposals or be impossible to reassemble.

An RFP response is a more detailed, formal version of a proposal—it contains more components around the details of the team, the process, the timeline, and the budget. Both the proposal and the RFP response should be kept clean and crisp. Your client does not have time to read extra words.

EXERCISE TWENTY-THREE
Map, Diagram, & Write a Response to an RFP

Your instructor will provide one for a particular company. If you're doing this book's exercises without an instructor, Google an RFP outline and respond to it. I'll say it one more time: Keep your language clean and crisp.

CHAPTER FOURTEEN

Copywriting

I T HAPPENS TO US ALL. Sooner or later, every designer ends up writing something for someone because the copy submitted is too awful to use or the copywriter has gone missing. Work on your skills, so you'll be up to the task. Copywriting can be extremely lucrative and can add another income stream to your bank account.

I believe a good writer can write anything, and it's important to think of advertising copywriting as just another string to your bow. Some extremely well-known writers of literature have quietly made a living by writing for business. As I recall, Colette supported herself for some time by writing advertising for a company that sold pearls. That's why pearls are so often mentioned in her novels.[89]

WHAT KIND OF COPY IS IT?

"Advertising" is a broad term: Consumer advertising is what you see on TV, on Spotify, on Facebook. Business-to-Business copywriting is—rather clearly—the advertising of one business to another. And a third kind of copywriting—although some writers might take umbrage at being classified in the advertising department—is writing for marketing communications, or "marcom." I lump

---

[89] "From the age of twelve, Gigi had known that Madame Otero's string of large black pearls were 'dipped,'—that is to say, artificially tinted—while the three strings of her matchlessly graded pearl necklace were worth 'a king's ransom'; that Madame de Pougy's seven rows lacked 'life'; that Eugénie Fougère's famous diamond bolero was quite worthless; and that no self-respecting woman gadded about, like Madame Antokolski, in a coupé upholstered in mauve satin." from *Gigi*, by Colette.

marcom in with copywriting in this book because it uses writing for a commercial purpose—supporting the brand.

FIRST, TARGETS

In order to write copy well, you must know exactly who your target is and write directly to that person. Did the design team create mood boards or personas? Get all the information you can about who will read your piece. If no research is to be had—which happens—do your own research. Ask your contact on the client side. Someone will know the basics about the product or business's target. Don't write before you know the advertising's demographics, at least.

BRUSH OFF YOUR POETRY HAT

I treat writing ad copy like writing poetry. Sometimes poems are long stories, sometimes they're haiku, sometimes they're intimations, sometimes they're blurts. Ad copy is like poetry because every word is much more thought through than the words in most prose, and because the words are strung together in ways that depend on (disguised) uses of rhythm and meter—often the meter of everyday speech. Brush off your poetry hat and employ the same use of mental focus, rhythm, and pacing that you use when writing poems. This will nudge you out of writing a style that is too flat and prosey for advertising. Time may be short, but don't let that bother you. Just don your earbuds and focus in on your words' rhythm and meter.

BE WISE ABOUT COPY OKAYS

As in designing, it's important to get clients in agreement about objectives early and to have them sign off on the direction and general tone of your written work before you begin writing. This is as true for three words of copy about a Prada shoe as it is about writing an entire software manufacturer's website. Make sure you get copy okays throughout the process—starting with ideation, in order that you don't get to the end of the process and hear, as my friend Tony once heard from a well-known clothing designer, "This isn't right. You don't understand. I'm blonde. It has to be more blonde."

WRITE ALONE

There is nothing worse than copy written by a committee. Brainstorming—that time-consuming and tedious practice—you can live through. Smile and look enthusiastic and let them cavort around putting up big sheets of ideas and starring things with highlighters. But then go to your desk, put in the earpods, and write the copy alone.

EXERCISE TWENTY-FOUR
Exercise Your Inner Colette

In thirty-five words, tell us why a thirty-two year-old American woman who works for a large publishing conglomerate, bikes to work, and lives with a thirty-seven-year-old partner should spend her next six paychecks on a perfectly matched three-strand pearl necklace. Channel your inner Colette.

CHAPTER FIFTEEN

Writing for Social Media

I T'S A TRUISM THAT WRITING FOR WEBSITES IS DIFFERENT FROM WRITING articles or advertisements. People, as I am sure you're aware, tend to scan sites rather than read them. Luckily, many of the writing techniques that we've been practicing in this book transfer very well to writing for the web. We've talked about writing in a simple, clear way. We've talked about using an informal tone. And I've pounded you repeatedly with the notion that you must always write with a specific reader in mind. Do all these things when writing for the web.

In the exercises, you've written various "who, what, when, where, why, and how" pieces. Do the same with the web: Put the most important thing you have to say right up front, in the first paragraph at the top. Try to get it all into one paragraph. Avoid having to write a second paragraph. Keep that paragraph on topic. Say only one thing. No long tracts that scroll for miles. Use bullet points for anything that can be made into a list. As we've mentioned before, and as Strunk and White have proclaimed for sixty years, "Use no unnecessary words." As you do in articles and papers, vary your sentence structure, and use the active voice rather than the passive voice. Instead of "The rose-tattoo-illustrated moustache cup was designed by Jessica," say, "Jessica designed the rose-tattoo-illustrated moustache cup."

Use headers in much the same way we've been using them in this book. Headers should be short and allow the reader to navigate the page quickly. Use a header for every third paragraph, more or less. Avoid acronyms, jargon, cheesiness, technical terminology, and avoid trying to sound breezy or younger than you are. Nothing worse than a forty-year-old copywriter trying to sound like a twenty-something. What a clank festival.

All in all, keep it short, pointed, specific, direct, and don't waste time welcoming people or explaining anything. If you must explain something technical or involved, provide links to technical pages or downloadable information. And make sure the tone is consistent throughout the site, including those technical pages.

CREATING A COHESIVE IDENTITY ONLINE

Even today, many clients don't have a cohesive identity across platforms. When designing, you know to guide the client in creating a seamless brand identity. But somehow this seamlessness ends at the designing. Often the tone of the website will be information-heavy and ponderous, the Facebook page spritely and excited-sounding, and the Twitter account aggressive. (I'd mention Instagram, but not a lot of writing there.)

Variety in tone breaks the voice of the brand, and it happens because different people have been assigned the updating of different parts of its online presence. If you're the writer on the project, try to get as many parts of the online presence under your wing as possible. Make sure that if anyone else is assigned to posting, they learn and have been able to capture the variations of tone you specify.

KEEP THE MUSIC PLAYING

One of the wonders of the post-postmodern world is that clients will spend thousands and thousands of dollars creating a new website; starting a blog; and opening Twitter feeds, Facebook pages, and Instagram accounts. Then, after the first few months, they slowly stop updating them.

Of all the important aspects of social media, adopting a regular posting schedule is the most crucial. If you don't refresh and remind, you don't exist. The occasional post is fine if you're a human with a personal site; it's anathema if you're a service business.

Refreshment can take many forms: product news, links to events, news about people, little tidbits of information and how-to's, links to podcasts created by the brand's leadership. But each kind of information must be treated as a separate asset, have its own piece of the brand story, and have its own schedule for deliverables and posting schedule. Apps like Hootsuite help manage this information, but these apps need significant human tending.

Whether you use an app to help you schedule or not, make sure, before you launch your social media effort, that you have a number of blog entries and Facebook posts in the bag, ready to post, so you don't have to take time, those first few days after the launch, creating new copy.

Invent a posting schedule for types of posts and create a calendar. Make sure the plan is updated regularly, and stay in close touch with your client-side team to glean ideas for posts about upcoming events, executive talks, and product launches. Maintaining a brand through social media is a team sport.

EXERCISE TWENTY-FIVE
Create a Social Media Plan

Since we don't have a client at the ready, you'll be the client.

Create a social media posting schedule for your design business.

What is your brand story? How will it play out in social media?

What do you plan to post, where, and when for the next three months?

Take everything into account: process and product news; information about events; tidbits and lore; podcast dates, times, and excerpts; upcoming holidays and seasons, and promotions around those holidays and seasons.

Create a mind map, find the rich club, make a diagram, and design a calendar and prompting system for yourself. Take a look social media marketing apps. Would they help you at this stage, or be too complex for your needs?

Writing Tips

— 1   Spellcheck and then reread for inappropriate words that the spellchecker may have substituted in Eros.

— 2   Even if you think you're way past this, make sure your sentences all have fully spelled-out words, a subject and a verb, a capital and a period. ur not texting

— 3   If you use more than five of someone else's words in succession—words they wrote, posted, or that you overheard in a café—credit that person, book, or site. Credit everything. Tell us who said it. This makes you look intelligent and thorough and willing to play in the writing playpen. Stealing is an end to your career as a writer. We have to trust you. (Unless you're an old Postmodernist, but nobody remembers the "untrustworthy narrator" anymore, so forget I said it.)

— 4   Read your writing aloud to your partner or to the dog. Don't let either critique your work—particularly the dog—but listen to yourself. Where there are pauses, there should be punctuation. Where you get bored with the drone of your own voice, take out those words. Where you're tempted to say "yada, yada," eliminate that idea. Real writing flows like spoken language, so turn on the tap.

— 5   Trash your thesaurus and promise to never use it again. Thesaurus-writing is obvious to a real reader, often featuring words in places where their exact meaning is a shade off and doesn't fit. Trust yourself and use the words that come to your mind.

— 6   Avoid clichés, stuffers, boring extra words, acronyms, text-lingo, and dumb pseudo-words that mean nothing in a sentence. Oscar Wilde said, "If I've ever heard a word, I don't use it." You don't have to go that far.

— 7 Don't pretend you and your reader are just lying around in robes watching TV and eating caramel corn. Sit up straight and act like your intelligent Aunt Josephine is visiting. Too sloppy, too familiar writing is unappealing: It is a pose.

— 8 Avoid using the verb "to be": as in, "He was," "I am," "she is," "they were." Instead, substitute an active verb: "she saw," "he ate," "we sniffled."

— 9 Chances are you don't have a PhD in rhetoric. So don't feel that you must puff up and prance around with big words and phrases. The smartest things are said in the fewest words. It takes guts to write short sentences.

— 10 Every time you make an assertion, back it up with a fact. "The landscapers in my neighborhood are often trilingual. Florence Dosono, my gardener, speaks Tagalog, English, and Spanish every day." Back up assertions with facts every time, don't just float on and on asserting yourself into the clouds, endlessly. That's what my Russian grandfather called "making heavenly biscuits." Including examples gives the reader a toe on the ground.

— 11 Don't try to figure out what you're trying to say while you're trying to say it. Don't have a couple beers and suddenly decide you're Dylan Thomas and let it all out on the page. You're not Dylan Thomas or any other Dylan so stick with sobriety. No one wants to read along as you chase around with a butterfly net hoping you'll find an idea. Find the idea. Write the idea. Go on to the next idea. Build them all into a nice little idea-pile in which they all relate, and then let the reader go home for lunch. It's juvenile to expect your readers to keep reading to sort out your nonexistent thinking for you. They won't sort. They'll stop reading.

Eleven Errors of Death

When my students give me papers or articles to read, they know that I will stop reading immediately if I run across one of these grammatical or stylistic errors. The paper then becomes a "dead draft" which they must revivify and turn in again.

— ERROR 1 *Being boring.*

Difficult ideas need to be presented in short, clear ways that do not sound like the drone of a didgeridoo. No one has the time: Watch your pacing.

— ERROR 2 *Being too clever.*

You are not a leprechaun. You are not a clown. A good funny moment is valuable, but pace them. Use them to open up your readers hearts and make them want to keep reading. Don't act like you're auditioning to be a late-night stand-up comic. Being too funny will undercut your thinking with a design audience, which is basically a sober, steeped-in-the-Bauhaus bunch of INFPs.

— ERROR 3 *Mixing up it's and its.*

It's a real problem. Because every word uses an apostrophe in its possessive except "it." It's → it is. Its → "something belonging to IT."
 Never forget this. Write it on your head.

— ERROR 4 *Not taking a stand on the Great Possessive Controversy.*

Up until very recently, grammarians did not believe that everyone had "their" baseball. Everyone had *his* baseball or everyone had *her* baseball—mostly, it must be admitted, "his" baseball—which reminded us all how gendered our language is.
 In the seventies, people started saying, "Everyone has *their* baseball," in order not to call attention to gender, and this was thoughtful, though it had grammar

buffs gagging for years. Not because of the gender issue, but because the idea of using a plural to mean something singular was a horror to the educated eardrum. It had something to do with the beauty of systems. I'll just leave it right there.

Recently, things have gotten to the point that "their" has been accepted by most publications, and even I have started to go along, though using the plural still makes me grind my teeth. However, something has recently given me a glimmer of hope for the future of the singular possessive.

In academia, gender-neutral language is gaining a footing, and a couple of options are gaining ground on the ubiquitous "their." The Spivak pronoun "eir" (the possessive of "e") can be used as an alternative to "his and hers." And the gender-neutral "hir" (the possessive of "ze") is also vying for the title. I'd be more inclined to use "hir," probably because it doesn't start with an "e," which sounds odd to me.

You're going to have to take a stand and stick to it. If you get yourself into an "everyone" tangle and don't want to use "their," make everything plural or, if you want to be inclusive yet use a singular possessive, use "hir." Everyone has hir baseball. I dare anyone to fault you.

— ERROR 5 *Declining the verbs "to lay" or "to lie" incorrectly.*

These are two separate, completely different verbs, but they look alike in some conjugations and so there's much confusion about them. The quickest way to show you cannot write is to use lay or lie incorrectly. This is the deal:

	TO LIE	TO LAY
Present	I lie down.	I lay the book on the table.
Past	I lay down.	I laid the book on the table.
Present Perfect	I have lain down.	I have laid the book on the table.

When do you use "lay" and when "lie"? You lay an object down. (That's where "getting laid" comes from, it's about objects, not lovers.) But a person lies down—anything that has control over its own body lies down. When you're in control of something, you lay it down.

The words, "Now I lay me down to sleep" seem confusing. But in them, the person speaking is using the verb "to lay," not "to lie." The speaker is treating herself as an object, and for this reason she uses "to lay" instead of using "to lie," and saying, "Now I'm lying down to sleep." Laying yourself down to sleep is archaic usage, so don't use it unless praying.

Again: You lay an object down. A person lies down. So does a dog.

When you command your dog, teach her to "lie down." ("Lay down" is grammatically incorrect and lord knows we can't have dogs responding to ungrammatical commands.)

— ERROR 6   *The biggest grammatical problem plaguing design academics today: Confusing the pronouns for subject and object.*

Somehow, design academics get the idea that "me" is not as elegant a word as "I," and they try to use "I" everywhere. This is sad and wrong. "I" is a subject, not an object. "Please give the information to him and me." It sounds wrong to the *uneducated* ear. But it's *right*. If I catch you telling people to give the information to "he and I," I will come after you. Generally, if you're using the word "to" at the end of a sentence and plan to use a pronoun, use "him," "her," "hir," "them," or "me."

The *only* time this is not true is when the verb of the sentence is the verb "to be." When your friend asks who's at the door, you can say "It is I." You'll dazzle with your grasp of the irregular. But generally: He gave it to me; he gave it to him; he threw it to her and me. Give the proposal to Joe and **me**. Always put yourself last. Get used to the sound of it.

— ERROR 7   *Mixing up "effect" and "affect."*

Each is used two ways. "Affect" is generally used as a verb. (He affected his students.) "Effect" is generally used as a noun. (It had a strange effect.) The confusion comes because psychologists use the term "affect" as a noun, (He had no affect—he was as dull as an electric dryer.) and "effect" is sometimes used as a verb (He effected change. He was a veritable tornado of innovation.) But 99 percent of the time you'll use the first two.

— ERROR 8   *Mixing up "nauseated" and "nauseous."*

A color is nauseous. You feel nauseated. Unless you have the effect of making people nauseated when they see you. Then you're nauseous.

— ERROR 9   *Using clichés.*

Using clichés tells the reader that you're willing to repeat words you have heard without evaluating what they mean. This leads us to believe that you do not make a habit of examining thoughts or ideas before you adopt and repeat them. Before you use words, examine them as though they are a glass from which you plan to drink. Never say you're "passionate" about anything or I will kill you in a sudden fit of rage. Never "unpack" a notion. Nobody wants to hire a parrot.

— ERROR 10   *Making nouns into verbs, or verbs into nouns.*

The dictionary will include anything in the common parlance. Just because a word is in the dictionary does not mean it's a good word. It may just be a cheesy word that's used a lot.

Do not "craft" writing. "Crafting" in general has an aroma of hobby stores and plastic bead kits. Writers write, they do not craft.

Do not "onboard" anything. "Onboard" is not a verb.

Do not "otherize" anything or anyone, or claim to have been "otherized."

A book is not a "good read." ("Read" is not a noun.) "It is a good book," will suffice. You do not "journal." You write in a journal. (This is one of my editor's pet peeves.)

Do not "utilize" anything. Just use it.

And, if you want to kill two birds with one stone, don't "leverage" anything. "Leverage" is a noun, and it's also business speak. Don't use it.

Nobody "gifted" you with anything. Do not "gift" anything. Just give it. "Gifting" puts the focus on the giver rather than on the gift. The implicit connotation is, "How wonderful I am that I am bestowing this fruit basket upon you."

— ERROR 11   *Using business-speak.*

Do not "reach out" to people when you mean you're emailing to ask them a question. Do not refer to your group's "core competency," when you mean its fundamental strength. Avoid "buying in"—just agree. Don't "drill down" unless you're in the oil business. And make sure that if the item you're describing is "robust," it's coffee, not your operating system.

Don't say you're "looking to transition into the social impact design space," when you want to say that you'd like to change jobs and make design that helps people.

Deflate your prose. Stick a knife in the tire. Readers will love you for it.

How to Get It All Read

I can't tell you how many times some nice designer has come up to me and said, "I just loved your book. I can't really remember what it was about, but I loved it while I was reading it." They really say that. There's nothing a writer likes better than becoming part of the confused cultural haze that clouds your world.

Epictetus once said, "If you would be a reader, read; if a writer, write." But in my experience, the best writers read. A lot. And good designers read a lot, too. How to do it? There's the rub. We live, we work, we commute, we cook, we take care of children, we see friends. When are we supposed to read—when do we have the time to focus and really understand what we're reading?

Luckily for you, I have accumulated a pocketful of tricks for getting more reading done. Here they are:

— 1 *Never read anything you don't want to read.*

This may seem obvious, but it is amazing how much junk is forced on you that you do not have to read. People with moist eyes press books into your hands.

They say, "It's about living in the moment in the eternal Now and it changed my life!"

I say skip it.

Read only what you want to read, be it graphic novel or Uline catalog. Because if you only read what you want to read, you will never avoid reading, and it will become as natural to you as breathing in and out in the eternal Now.

— 2 *Avoid any book that has the words "Syndrome," "Plan," "Secret," or "The Story of" in the title.*

Also avoid any book that describes the protagonist as uncovering, hunting, taking control of, communicating (with dogs), targeting (for death), taking on

159

(a new assignment), or discovering (devastating secrets). You really just do not have the time.

— 3 *Similarly, avoid books that feature:*

> a rogue CIA agent
> a lethal teenage gang
> a vampire summit
> a gangster patient
> combinations of the above

— 4 *Read the introduction to an academic work before reading the work itself.*

Then, if you're interested, read the piece. Read the original writer before reading any sort of commentary on that writer. For instance, Carl Jung is a far better writer than most of the people who comment on him. Just cut to the chase and read him in the original. I read all academic works in the tub. That way, if I get bored with the formal prose, I tend to keep reading to the end, because it's more work to get out and dry off than it is to finish the piece.

— 5 *Read aloud.*

I remember being terribly jealous years ago when Margaret Visser told me that she and her husband took turns reading to each other from ancient Greek tracts while doing the dishes in the evening. How cultured is that? My jealousy knew no bounds. But a few years later I was able to steal their routine. I recommend having your partner read to you from the *Odyssey* while your hands are submerged in the suds. (Not the Iliad. Too much martialing of troops.) This practice, day in and day out, is satisfying. And will get you through the Saint John's Reading List at a slow, yet steady pace.[90]

— 6 *Read happy things on the way to work.*

I include the design blogs, *Communication Arts* and *Metropolis* magazine in the happy zone. I feel happy looking at all the bright colors and seeing that soon everything is going to be nice and environmental and green and that everyone will soon have attractive lamps and tile.

---

90 https://www.sjc.edu/academic-programs/undergraduate/seminar/annapolis-undergraduate-readings, (Accessed 11 June, 2018)

— 7   *Read the news at lunch.*

If lunch is filled with clients and prospecting, read the news in the morning right when you get in and everyone else is getting in late and talking about what a line there was at Starbucks. It's amazing how long morning office-settling takes, and you can be done with it before they're ready to go.

— 8   *Read anything with the word "Journal," "Newsletter," or "Update" in the title on the way back from work.*

That's if you travel by public conveyance or shuttle. Commuting solo by car will have to go if you're going to get your reading done.

— 9   *Have only one book on your bedside table.*

Read before sleep or if worried. Avoid anything with an exciting plot. I find that a nice long mid-eighteenth century novel does the trick. The Russians are also great for plots that unfold in real time. Tolstoy yes. Lermontov yes. Dostoyevsky no, because he'll rile you up too much and have you thinking about the damned questions and so forth.

— 10   *Save reading the work of the French post-structuralists for times when you have had red wine or caffeine by accident and it's kept you up.*

These are probably similar conditions to those under which it was written.

LAST THOUGHTS

M Y GOSH. HERE WE ARE, AT THE END OF THE BOOK. It all went so fast. Only yesterday we were knee-deep in academic writing. And now we've dashed through tips and tricks. Since we're here, let me pull back from all those listings, and say something serious.

"Dare to declare who you are." That's what the great Hildegard of Bingen said, and I think about it often. Dare to say what you have to say in life. It's all over so fast, and you don't want to lie there on the old deathbed and think, "I had a talent for writing, but I never got to it because people thought of me as a designer."

You have to show people your writing talent in order for them to understand that you're a designer who can write. They will assume that you can't, because in our industrialized world, people are only supposed to be good for one thing. Prove them wrong. I know that if you've worked through all the exercises and memorized the tips in this book, you've learned to write better than most of the people who call themselves writers. So, show people who you are. When you can write well and design well, you've doubled the ways you can make things in this world. Making things makes for happiness. So, here's to you, and to your double happiness.

ILLUSTRATION NOTES
Compiled by Robert Baxter

fig 1.A

In 1929, after Picasso turned down a commission to create the frontispiece for James Joyce's *Tales of Shem and Shaw*, Constantin Brâncuşi took up the project. First making a naturalistic portrait, Brancusi then refined his experience of Joyce to symbolic representation. *The Symbol of James Joyce* is a composition made up of three lines, a small scrawl of script, and a broken spiral, which Joyce himself called "a whirligig."[91] That spiral is reproduced here to show the way that a composition which at first seems chaotic may be supported by a disciplined structure working behind the scenes.

fig 2.1

In 1949, Charles K. Bliss created his Blissymbols, a form of *semantography*, intending the system of pictographs, ideographs, and their relational "grammar" as a visual language that could jump national boundaries. A few hundred unique Blisscharacters represent concise objects or ideas. The downward-sloping diagonal at the beginning of our illustration's second line refers to a pen or pencil and signifies "writing." Blisscharacters can also be combined into Blisswords, which hold more complex meanings. The downward-facing semi-circle with an arrow in the illustration's first line symbolizes "mind + down," something coming from the mind: an "idea". This same "mind" semicircle appears in the second line, but now floats above a flat triangle, the symbol for "making," and creates the word for "design." The longer Blissword in the middle of the illustration has a small venn-diagram shape on either side, which indicates that the word is created by the user. Our illustrated combination of "generalized + thinking (descriptor) + structure," which we created specifically for this text, stands for the word "systematized."

People who are non-speaking, have limited literacy, or need to communicate across language barriers still often use Blissymbolics. We first found it referenced in Henry Dreyfuss's *Symbol Sourcebook* (1972). Blissymbolics Communication International, or BCI, maintains the language.[92]

fig 2.2

Gregg Shorthand is a stenographic script used to transcribe speech rapidly. Though a professional typist can record 75–120 words

---

91 For more information, see Halpar, Nathan. "Joyce and Brancusi: The Brancusi Portrait." In *Joyce & Paris 1902... 1920–1940... 1975 (version Anglaise): Papers from the Fifth International James Joyce Symposium, Paris, 16–20 June 1975*, edited by Jacques Aubert and Maria Jolas, 69–78. Vol. 2. Presses Univ. Septentrion, 1979.

92 You'll find more information at http://www.blissymbolics.org/.

per minute, a skilled stenographer can write more than 200 words per minute. Such speed is possible because shorthand is actually another visual language, a variant of English optimized for speed. Its alphabet transcribes a simplified phonetic system and its characters use a limited set of strokes to streamline the writing process. With the advent of audio recording and voice recognition, shorthand has gradually fallen from common use. But it's still a useful and highly functional language and a fascinating artifact of semantic adaptation driven by industrial requirements.

fig 2.3
In the 1840s, Englishman Isaac Pitman invented a widely-used method of shorthand, for which he was later knighted by Queen Victoria. A founder of England's Vegetarian Society (considered a bizarre practice at the time), Pitman was a perfectionistic genius. Very much under the influence of his rapidly industrializing society's desire for increased speed and efficiency, Pitman invented a spelling system that aimed to reproduce all the sounds of English in a systematic way, avoiding such confusing spelling horrors as "though," and "through." His essentialized spelling system proved so popular that it became the model for The International Phonetic Alphabet, or IPA, a system of 163 different symbols (letters, diacritics, and prosodic marks) used to represent the vast spectrum of sounds in human speech. Although this phonetic system is built around the sounds of Romance languages (those stemming from Latin) it is meant to be "language agnostic." You may recognize parts of the IPA from your use of dictionary entries and translation guides.

fig 2.4
Russian is an East Slavic language of the Indo-European family. It's traced from the language of the Kievan Rus', a group of East Slavic tribes who had such trouble fighting over who was going to rule that in 862 they finally asked an outsider, a Viking named Rurik, to govern them. This was the beginning of Russia as we know it.

When creating an alphabet to symbolize their newly shared language, the Rus' based most of their character set on Greek uncial script, but added some letters and ligatures from the Glagolitic alphabet. (Created by Byzantine brothers Cyril and Methodius to write Old Church Slavonic, the Glagolitic alphabet includes letters for sounds not found in Greek. This invention earned them Orthodox sainthood.) Russian's glyph mash-up of Greek and Glagolitic is quite different from the less blended set of signifiers used to write English and the Romance languages, which are written with Roman characters modified from the Cumean Greek. Russian also differs from these languages typographically: The characters have a square basis, with few ascenders and descenders.

fig 3.1
Although the words with the greatest number of synonyms tend to be euphemisms—we could have spent our time illustrating "pushing up the daisies," "biting the dust," "buying the farm" or "falling off the perch"—we wanted something with a bit more connotative range. Our little doodle of Auguste Rodin's *The Thinker* perches upon our list of person-words because a reference to Rainer Maria Rilke's *Letters to a Young Poet* appears on the preceding page.

In these letters, Rilke talks about what it is to be a truly thinking, feeling, living person, and passes on much of what he learned while a student of Rodin. At the end of the second letter he muses: "If I were to say who has given me the greatest experience of the essence of creativity, its depths and eternity, there are just two names would mention: Jacobsen, that great, great poet, and Auguste Rodin, the sculptor, who is without peer among all artists who are alive today."[93]

---

93   Rilke, Rainer Maria and Kappus, Franz Xaver. *Letters to a Young Poet*, in an edition by M.D. Herter Norton (translator). (New York: W.W. Norton & Co., 1993).

fig 4.A

In the Reed-Kellogg system of sentence diagramming, subjects and predicates sit on a horizontal line with a vertical bar dividing them. Modifiers, written on diagonals, extend down from this line. With six clear subject/predicate relationships, numerous modifiers, and a sequence of prepositions and conjunctions, our sentence is evidently a bit complicated.

fig 4.B

Children just beginning to learn about grammar once studied the "phonetics" curriculum, a basic form of sentence diagramming. They learned to underline subjects, the static part of a sentence, and to put a dynamic zig-zag line under predicates, the active component. This was a curious instance of grammatical symbol making, very much in step with modernist analysis of the line.

fig 4.1

We rendered Woolf's excerpt using a notation method outlined in Dwight Bolinger's *Intonation and Its Parts: Melody in Spoken English*.[94] The baseline of each syllable (or sometimes of individual letters) shifts to mimic the way the speaker's voice may slip through pitch when speaking a sentence aloud. Other methods of documenting intonation exist (usually employed for understanding pitch shifts between statement, question, and demand in other languages), but Bolinger's has the most dynamic range, and we found the result to be far more visually interesting than those of our alternatives.

fig 6.1

$1/2$ The first recorded flow chart can be found in a 1921 publication of the American Society of Mechanical Engineers: *Process Charts*, presented by Frank B. Gilbreth and I. M. Gilbreth. "Every detail of a process is more or less affected by every other detail; therefore the entire process must be presented in such form that it can be visualized all at once before any changes are made in any of its subdivisions."[95] We constructed our illustration using a chart from this paper as a guide.

$2/2$ This is the molecular structure of Copper Pthalocyanine ($C_{32}H_{16}CuN_8$), known more commonly as the pigment Pthalo Blue. (We would have liked to use IKB 79, Yves Klein Blue, but its structure is somewhat more complex, and, to the untrained-eye, would not have read very well as the "molecular diagram" described in the text.)

fig 7.1

We spent time trying to find the appropriate historical reference on which to develop our tree diagramming method.

Unfortunately, tree diagrams for writing tend toward the extreme — fully abstract sketches on one end, and non-visual numbered lists on the other. Neither is quite representative enough for our purposes, so we defined our own symbols. The *claim* (eventually the *thesis*) creates a shape, but leaves it hollow; it is an outline without substance. The *reason* hammers that assertion into a simple shape, and the *example* fills it in. The *conclusion*, in the end, takes the same shape as the initial *claim*, but through the course of the *argument* has been filled in.

fig 7.B

We derived this little sample tree from Michael Beirut's essay, "Why Designers Can't Think."[96] Though it doesn't conform perfectly to the five-paragraph tree, it does have three convenient branches of argument: *process*,

---

94 Bolinger, Dwight. *Intonation and Its Parts: Melody in Spoken English*. Redwood City, CA: Stanford University Press, 1986.

95 Gilbreth, Frank B. and I. M. Gilbreth. *Process Charts: First Steps in Finding the One Best Way to Do Work*. New York, NY: The American Society of Mechanical Engineers, 1921. 15.

96 Beirut, Michael. "Why Designers Can't Think," in *Seventy-Nine Short Essays on Design*, 14–17. New York, NY: Princeton Architectural Press, 2007.

product, and literacy. Beirut draws a clear linear relationship between his introduction and his conclusion, which is an admirable thing and quite valuable for our purposes.

fig 7.8

You can grow infinitely many kinds of tree essays. Our arboretum holds a few. Consider these: the many-branched tree, with more than three component arguments; the example-collection tree, with each branch listing a sequence of many instances of occurrence; the question/answer tree, which begins with a question in the thesis paragraph and answers that question in the conclusion. Why is a tree not a house? Tree arguments are linear, relatively stable and non-cyclical. The only loop they make is the repetition of the thesis idea—reworded—as conclusion.

fig 7.9

In the conclusion of his longform essay *On the Spiritual in Art*, Wassily Kandinsky outlines his ideas on the relationship between the melodic and symphonic.[97] To exemplify a "melodic composition with plain rhythm," he references Cezanne's *Bathing Women*, also known as *The Bathers*. Oppositely, to exemplify "those new symphonic compositions," he shows reproductions of many of his own pieces, including *Composition No. 4 (Oil)*, also known as *Impression V (Park)*. These two works form the basis of our diagram, with the skeleton of each outlining its principle form, the central triangle.

Fig 7.10

Though the entirety of the Eames House[98] would have made a wonderful idea-house diagram, for the sake of brevity we have focused on the living section of the ground floor. Not pictured are the courtyard, upstairs bedrooms and bathrooms, and connected studio area. We've resized some doorways a bit here and there to unify this house with the diagrams in the following illustrations. The décor is pieced together from various historic photos including the blackbird of "chair advertisement" infamy.[99]

fig 7.12

Our idea-house is built from Beatrice Warde's *The Crystal Goblet*, in which she presents the modernist argument for invisible typography. We reviewed a number of different options for this house, considering and rejecting F. T. Marinetti's *Manifesto of Futurism* and Aleksandr Rodchenko's *Who We Are: Manifesto of the Constructivist Group*, both of which proved—ironically—too linear.[100] Warde's essay has a very simple, yet distinct, non-linear structure that works well for picturing the form of a semi-lattice essay. The diagram itself is structured (loosely) around the form of a Gothic cathedral. The narthex symbolizes the introduction; the nave, crossing, choir, and apse hold the essential arguments; the two side-aisles model the gold/crystal parallel, and a lopsided transept houses the idea of modernism.

fig 7.13

To demonstrate the variety of semi-lattice structures, we turned to various construction patterns from different cultures. Alternative treatments of thought/writing/space are reflected in these buildings.

¼ A section of the Acropolis complex in Athens, Greece (seventh through fifth century BCE) with the statue of *Athena Promachos*

97 Kandinsky, Wassily. *On the Spiritual in Art*, 96–99. New York, NY: Solomon R. Guggenheim Foundation, 1946.

98 Historic American Buildings Survey, Creator, Charles Eames, Ray Eames, Kenneth Acker, Eero Saarinen, Edgardo Contini, Lucia Eames, et al. *Eames House, 203 Chautauqua Boulevard, Los Angeles, Los Angeles County, CA*. California, Los Angeles, Los Angeles County, 1933. Documentation Compiled After Photograph. https://www.loc.gov/item/ca4169/.

99 Eames, Charles and Ray Eames. *An Eames Anthology*. Edited by Daniel Ostroff. New Haven, CT: Yale University Press, 2015.

100 Warde, Beatrice. (1930) 2009. *The Crystal Goblet, or Why Printing Should Be Invisible*. 1956. In *Graphic Design Theory: Readings from the Field*, edited by Helen Armstrong, 39–43. New York, NY: Princeton Architectural Press. The two manifestos can also be found in Helen Armstrong's collection if you would like to read them.

central. Le Corbusier references this section in *Towards a Modern Architecture* after a discussion of the *plan*: "the plan bears within itself a primary and pre-determined rhythm: the work is developed in extent and in height following the prescriptions of the plan, with results which can range from the simplest to the most complex, all coming within the same law. Unity of law is the law of a good plan: a simple law capable of infinite modulation."[101]

²⁄₄ The church of St Louis des Invalides in Paris (17th century CE), by Jules Hardouin-Mansart. "The interior, except for the oval chancel, is more academically balanced, that is, less dynamic in its spatial relations that the works of Hardouin-Mansart's predecessors. But the dome is constructed so that in looking up one sees through a wide opening in the inner cupola on to the painted surface of a second cupola, lit by concealed windows—a wholly Baroque spatial effect."[102]

³⁄₄ A cluster of Iglulik structures on the Melville Peninsula, documented by Danish archaeologist and anthropologist Therkel Mathiassen in 1922. This group contains "two living units plus rooms for clothing, dog harnesses, a meat locker, and a dog kennel."[103]

⁴⁄₄ The Nendrum Monastery[104] in Northern Ireland (sixth–eighth centuries CE) has been heavily stylized for this illustration, with the irregular concentric cashels fashioned into perfect circles.

fig 7.D

In his essay "I Come to Bury Graphic Design, Not to Praise It," Kenneth FitzGerald conducts a two-part investigation. First, he examines the goals of the design profession—both stated and behavioral. Woven into his discussion are thoughts on public betterment, modernism, elitism, and the vernacular. Second, he builds a critique of design education upon the foundation he's just poured. "An education *through* design rather than *in* design should be our goal. If that's not possible, what does it say for all the claims of design's significance to and in the world? Is design just for designers?"[105] Our house outline is a simplified map of the first part of his argument. We have omitted some of his important textual nodes/rooms that explore nuances of "undesign," Edward Tufte's information design, Richard Hollis's histories, "outside celebrity" via Rem Koolhaus and Dave Eggars, and movements toward the vernacular described by Robin Kinross.

fig 8.1

A version of this fable is recorded in *Chinese Fables and Folk Stories*, an early collection of English translations published in 1908.[106] The story explores the persuasive modes *ethos* and *pathos*. The lion assumes that his kingly character will convince the mosquitoes that he is right. Yet, as he is dying, he laments his arrogance and its resultant outcome: his use of the wrong method of persuasion has led to his downfall. "My pride and anger have brought me this fate. Had I used gentle words, the mosquitoes might have given me water for my thirst. I was wise and strong in the wilderness, and even the greatest of the animals feared my power. But I fought with the mosquitoes and I die — not because I have not strength to overcome, but because of the foolishness of anger."

fig 8.2

Clear documentation on this fable is hard to find—we discovered it in a Putnam Capricorn paperback called *Various Fables from Various*

101 Le Corbusier. Translated by Frederick Etchells. *Towards a Modern Architecture*. New York, NY: Praeger, 1960. 47–48, 50.

102 Pevsner, Nikolaus. *An Outline of European Architecture*. Great Britain: Penguin Books, 1966. 322–324.

103 Easton, Robert and Peter Nabokov. *Native American Architecture*. Oxford, England: Oxford University Press, 1990. 197.

104 Pevsner, Nikolaus. *An Outline of European Architecture*. Great Britain: Penguin Books, 1966. 41.

105 FitzGerald, Kenneth. "I Come to Bury Graphic Design, Not to Praise It." In *Emigre No. 66: Nudging Graphic Design*, edited by Rudy VanderLans. New York, NY: Princeton Architectural Press, 2004. 29–41.

106 Davis, Mary Hayes, and Chow-Leung. *Chinese Fables and Folk Stories*. New York, NY: American Book Co., 1908. 176–180.

Places which credits it as an African folktale.[107] Elsewhere it has been attributed more specifically to West Africa, and is bundled with many tales of Anansi the spider. We have omitted from our summary an additional bit of cleverness: when the Leopard and Jackal approach, the Ram, at the suggestion of his wife, pinches their young Lamb—the Leopard mistakes the Lamb's indignant cries for cries of hunger.

fig 8.3

We found the most complete documentation of this story in Orson Welles's script for *Mr. Arkadin*, written in 1954, but it certainly predates that publication. Variations have been found in later versions of the Indian *Panchatantra* (Bidpai) and in the Babylonian Talmud. The story has lived many lives and housed many different morals, with the Scorpion sometimes replaced with a Mouse, and the Frog replaced with a Tortoise or Turtle. In an earlier version, the Scorpion tries to sting his partner, but fails and is drowned. In another, attributed to Aesop, the Frog is the original aggressor and drowns his rider unprovoked, at which point a Kite scoops them both from the water, proving that treachery will be repaid with treachery.

fig 9.1

McLuhan makes this point as he begins a section discussing the relationship between the "unified pictorial space of Gutenberg culture" and contemporary society's "heterogeneity of tone and attitude."[108]

fig 10.3

This divided map analyses the well-known debate between Jan Van Toorn and Wim Crouwel at the Stedelijk Museum in Amsterdam on November 9, 1972, which was held on the occasion of an exhibition of Van Toorn's work.

Rick Poyner describes the debate: "If we reduce the two men's arguments to their most elementary form ... then Crouwel believes that it is the graphic designer's sacred duty to present what the client, as message-maker, wants to say, and to do this as clearly and objectively as possible.... For Van Toorn, this technician-like posture of detachment is an illusion. He argues that there can be no such thing as an objective message and no neutrality on the part of the designer, because any act of design, in which the designer takes the role of intermediary, will introduce an element of subjectivity." The debate has been quite beautifully preserved in English in a little orange volume published by the Monacelli Press.[109]

107 Di Prima, Diane, editor. *Various Fables from Various Places.*
New York, NY: G. P. Putnam's Sons, 1960. 59–60.

108 McLuhan, Marshall. *The Gutenberg Galaxy.* Toronto, Canada: University of Toronto Press, 1962. 135.

109 Crouwel, Wim and Jan Van Toorn. *The Debate: The Legendary Contest of Two Giants of Graphic Design.*
New York, NY: The Monacelli Press, 2015. 9, 19–42.

Index